Supply Networks in Developing Countries

Supply Networks in Developing Countries: Sustainable and Humanitarian Logistics in Growing Consumer Markets

BY

Tatenda Talent Chingono
University of Johannesburg, South Africa

And

Charles Mbohwa
University of Johannesburg, South Africa

United Kingdom – North America – Japan – India – Malaysia – China

Emerald Publishing Limited
Howard House, Wagon Lane, Bingley BD16 1WA, UK

First edition 2023

British Library Cataloguing in Publication Data
A catalogue record for this book is available from the British Library

ISBN: 978-1-80117-195-3 (Print)
ISBN: 978-1-80117-194-6 (Online)
ISBN: 978-1-80117-196-0 (Epub)

INVESTOR IN PEOPLE

Contents

List of Figures and Tables

Figures

Tables

Foreword

The book discusses research-based and evidence based upcoming issues in humanitarian logistics. These include new disaster occurrences, frameworks, and policies, the fourth industrial revolution, information technology, reverse logistics, supply chain modelling, and blockchains, and how these might be used to improve logistics for aid in underdeveloped nations. In light of the rising number of emergencies, as well as the complexity and size of international emergency disaster operations, it analyses challenges with the management of the humanitarian supply chains.

It presents research results on the logistics involved in providing humanitarian aid in light of the complexity and scope of emergencies and disasters that are growing. This book uses the research findings to propose the skills and information necessary to manage supply chains in both unpredictable and challenging contexts. It similarly further discusses the roles and duties of key stakeholders, including the victims of disasters, donors, relief agencies, non-governmental organisations (NGOs), governments, the military, the private sector, shipping/logistics companies, and academia. It outlines the duties and tasks of government agencies, NGOs, and academic institutions in preparing the various stakeholders with the information and abilities necessary to save lives in disasters and uncertain environments.

In circumstances that are frequently volatile, dangerous, unexpected, and unstable, supply chain management plays a crucial role in disaster planning and response. Insightful evidence-based advice and discussion of the major problems facing practitioners handling the logistics of disaster relief are provided in the book. It also based on broad literature review and research results, contains recommendations for best practices and global viewpoints on the nature of the logistical challenge facing humanitarians and the victims of the disaster.

Additionally, it suggests solutions for waste management and reverse logistics in times of disaster. This book is essential reading for all researchers and experts who need to understand and research on supply change management in times of emergencies. The main focusses identified in the research monograph is the need to pay attention to cooperation, coordination, and information exchange as three of the largest issues facing the humanitarian sector. Each chapter stands alone as a research chapter and connects its information to the supply chain as a whole. This makes it simple for the reader to select relevant chapters and get useful results that can contribute to their work.

Chapter 1

Humanitarian Logistics, Identifying and Reacting to Disasters

1.1. Introduction

The research trends and findings in the field of humanitarian logistics will be reviewed in this chapter. This review will explain how development help and relief during disasters and emergencies are delivered while focussing on case studies in humanitarian logistics and aid during disasters and crises. Humanitarian supply networks' diversity and complexity are reflected in humanitarian logistics.

The development of the application of theoretical ideas in supply chain management and commercial logistics also serves as a backdrop for the discussion of the experience of the Developing World. The point being made is that the complex environment in which humanitarian interventions take place in the Developing World presents serious management and leadership challenges due to the variety of disasters that can occur there, to political and cultural diversity, to the inadequate and inadequately maintained infrastructure, as well as other resource requirements needed to support and manage humanitarian interventions in a sustainable manner.

Additionally, the effectiveness, efficiency, and success of interventions are influenced by the participation of continental, regional, international, civil society organisations, global humanitarian agencies, and opinion leaders, who also control the level of cooperation and collaboration. A multitude of actors and the complexity of humanitarian supply networks in the Developing World, like everywhere, present significant leadership and logistical management issues.

1.2. Humanitarian Logistic Background Review

There hasn't been a lot of in-depth research on supply chain management and humanitarian logistics. One can see certain holes and that it is still developing. It has mostly focussed on integrating logistics best practices from the private and commercial sectors and working out how to incorporate them into supply chains for humanitarian purposes. Numerous researchers, including Tomasini and Van Wassenhove (2005), have published in this field of study. Some even

Supply Networks in Developing Countries:
Sustainable and Humanitarian Logistics in Growing Consumer Markets, 1–17
Copyright © 2023 by Tatenda Talent Chingono and Charles Mbohwa
Published under exclusive licence by Emerald Publishing Limited
doi:10.1108/978-1-80117-194-620231001

concentrate on the logistical tasks that multinational organisations can genuinely execute while aiding sizable non-governmental organisations (NGOs) in humanitarian efforts. Mbohwa (2008) explains how major NGOs, such as the Red Cross, United Nations International Children's Emergency Fund (UNICEF), and the World Food Programme (WFP), operate in Zimbabwe. He also identifies issues and offers remedies. The majority of research has concentrated on finding ways to reduce expenses while accelerating rescue efforts. Among others, they include Kleindorfer and Van Wassenhove (2004), Clark and Culkin (2007), Thompson (2008), Qiang, Nagurney, and Dong (2008), Van Wassenhove (2006), Thomas (2003b).

Thus, it is clear that there is a need for more research on improving supply chain systems, implementing green and reverse logistics, and exploring how the technologies of the Fourth Industrial Revolution may improve the efficacy of humanitarian operations. The effectiveness of logistics can also be measured in another study, and efforts can be made to make them as efficient and quick as feasible. As a result, there is still more work to be done in this area, notably implementation.

Humanitarian logistics can be fairly complex, thus it's surprising that manual techniques are still largely preferred over digital and quicker technologies. The majority of information technology (IT) resources are not being leveraged in a way that will increase and improve information availability, reporting, and learning (Thomas & Kopczak, 2005). Only a few assistance organisations, according to the research, have made an attempt to reduce humanitarian costs by developing high-performing logistics and supply chain operations. Since external conditions and the structure of funding have led to operations with high personnel turnover rates, dispersed technology, ill-defined manual processes, and a lack of institutional learning over time, it may be beyond the control of the majority of aid organisations. As a result, relief efforts are not as efficient, quick, or successful as they could be, and aid does not always reach victims (Thomas & Kopzack, 2005).

1.3. Humanitarian Supply Chains

The term 'humanitarian supply chain' refers to the network formed by the exchange of goods, services, money, and information between donors, recipients, suppliers, and other branches of humanitarian organisations with the aim of delivering tangible aid to recipients. Humanitarian supply chains may have features that don't normally belong in the category of humanitarian logistics. Non-logistics programme units are often in charge of maintaining contacts with donors, conducting needs analyses, arranging for the necessary supplies, and monitoring and assessing the effects of distributed resources. Units that implement programmes, manage funds with donors, oversee budgets, and coordinate activities with logistical units are all part of the humanitarian supply chain (Thomas & Kopzack, 2005).

The concept of humanitarian supply networks is based on the idea that disasters are becoming more common in the globe, necessitating the adoption and adaption of business and military supply network ideas and practices in response to humanitarian operations. All nations and continents are impacted by this, and Africa is no exception. Many humanitarian calamities overwhelm the community's ability to respond, pushing it beyond its breaking point and rendering the status quo systems ineffective. As a result, the communities will be vulnerable and in need of outside help (Thomas & Kopzack, 2005).

Man-made disasters are more common in emerging nations. However, natural disasters can also occur and have a substantial negative impact on the region's physical infrastructure by destroying bridges, airports, and other forms of electrical and transportation infrastructure. Agile supply networks must be present or engaged when this happens. It's crucial to focus on quick response times in these circumstances. This might be challenging in the Developing World, especially when there is inadequate infrastructure and slow communication. The planning horizon for slow-onset disasters is essential in these African environments to allow logisticians to focus on cost-efficiency (Oloruntoba & Gray, 2006).

Stakeholders are all the various parties that are involved with and impacted by this industry. These can be put into groups: UN agencies providing relief (WFP, UNICEF, etc.) and private corporate funders including Fritz Institute, Aidmatrix, and American logistics aid networks; public government donors including U.S. Agency for International Development (USAID), Department for International Development (DFID), and others; and NGOs including CARE, World Vision, and Oxfam.

Donors, aid organisations, NGOs, governments, military, and logistics service providers are all stakeholders of the humanitarian supply chain. They can collaborate and share information in efforts to assist victims of natural or man-made disasters (Thomas & Kopzack, 2005).

Distribution of food, water, sanitation, shelter, and medical assistance are typical areas of operation. Sponsors and suppliers make up the inbound sides. They may provide sponsorship in the form of money, gifts, grants, or supplies like food and non-food products. These progress downward in the supply chain as information travels both ways. Customers, also known as beneficiaries, communities, or projects, are divided between relief and development. Typically, there aren't any or very few logistics-related operations. Reverse logistics begin once the project is finished (mostly packaging materials and vehicles).

1.4. Characteristics of Humanitarian Logistics

- Ambiguous goals, with humanitarian efforts frequently being spontaneous, unsolicited, and desperate on the part of donors, agencies, the media, and beneficiaries.
- High uncertainty and complexity that depends on assessment of ongoing changes in supply and demand; limited resources with high employee turnover in staff with heavy physical and emotional demands, limited funding with challenges relating to cash flow, and frequently multiple damaged infrastructure.
- Humanitarian interventions after a disaster are typically characterised by acute urgency.
- A highly politicised environment, from donations through distribution in the field.

1.5. Humanitarian versus Commercial Supply Chains

- In contrast to commercial supply chains, which prioritise increasing profit and return on investment, humanitarian logistics prioritise yield in order to ensure that recipients receive the greatest possible benefit.
- Client pleasure in contrast to beneficiary survival.
- Deliberate volunteering as opposed to corporate social responsibility.
- Success rather than importance.

The three phases of operations are planning, quick reaction, and reconstruction. Planning entails risk management and disaster prevention.

Crisis management (short-term management) is the immediate response. Continuity and planning form the reconstruction (long-term management)

1.6. Humanitarian Supply Chains

There are several supply chains for various services, including development initiatives, food distribution, in-kind gift distribution, and emergency relief or response. Usually, there are four generic supply chains:

1. A supply chain with continuous replenishment enables easy management of very predictable demand from well-known customers (e.g. predictable regular supply of chronic medication).
2. Regular demand patterns, which are fairly predictable and forecastable, and lean supply chain (although might be seasonal). These put efficiency first (e.g. food distribution), possibly given the demand is understood from prior
3. Agile supply chain – typically ad hoc (may be the consequence of marketing campaigns, new product launches, promotions, or unanticipated possibilities). Consider the calculation for service cost (projects for development to adapt to unanticipated/unplanned demand).
4. Fully flexible supply chain – unpredicted and unpredictable demand brought on by unidentified consumers who have extraordinary or urgent needs (e.g. responding to the nature and incidence of disasters in Africa).

1.7. Disasters

Numerous disasters, including epidemics, floods, wildfires, storms, earthquakes, volcanic eruptions, and landslides, have struck the world during 2015. Inflicting a terrible toll on developing nations in particular, where disasters divert attention and resources away from the development that is urgently needed to escape poverty, these have claimed tens of thousands of lives, resulted in material losses in the billions of dollars, and caused terrible losses. In terms of logistics, supply chains, and humanitarian assistance, the cost of managing disasters has significantly increased. The United Nations' (UN) humanitarian appeal was

US$3.7 billion in 2005; by 2016, it had increased to almost US$20 billion (*The Guardian*, 2017).

Human activities frequently cause or at least exacerbate the calamities of today. A lack of suitable institutional and legislative systems, poor environmental management, and inadequate land-use planning all contribute to increased risk and multiplied effects of catastrophes, some of which are natural but some of which are caused by human activity. Under extreme environmental disaster scenarios, it is also predicted that the Human Development Index for sub-Saharan Africa will decline by as much as 24% by 2050, highlighting the need for resilient humanitarian logistics and supply management systems as well as mitigation and adaptation strategies. According to estimates, if this isn't done, there might be over a billion people living in extreme poverty in the region (UNDP, 2013).

African nations are exposed to a variety of disasters, including civil unrest, population mobility (refugees and internally displaced people), earthquakes, cyclones, flooding, droughts, and diseases (Chatora, 2005). Particularly in sub-Saharan Africa, the effects of the HIV/AIDS pandemic as well as the malaria and tuberculosis epidemics put downward pressure on sustainable development. Extreme weather and climatic events have become more common, particularly in West and Southern Africa, which has led to natural disasters said to be caused by climate change (IPCC, 2012).

Between 1994 and 2013, more than one billion people, or 25% of the world's population, were affected by dry spells, with 41% of the world's drought disasters occurring in Africa (UNISDR, 2015). Only 5% of all disasters, however, were drought-related and required humanitarian assistance. The Horn of Africa saw its worst drought in 60 years in 2011, putting more than 13.3 million people at risk of famine and malnutrition. Famine resulted from the drought in Somalia, where decades of conflict had worn down the nation's capacity to cope. This resulted in a significant increase in the need for humanitarian aid, necessitating efficient logistics and supply management to lessen the effects of the catastrophe in addition to preventive measures like the creation of irrigation systems (USAID, 2012).

Droughts frequently affect South Africa (WFF, 2016), and the nation is currently dealing with its worst drought in more than 35 years. This comes after several years of insufficient precipitation, the worst of which was in 2015, since 1904. As a result of the ongoing decline in dam levels brought on by the lack of rainfall in 2016, numerous cities nationwide were left almost completely dry. As a result, many South African provinces were labelled 'states of calamity' due to the drought.

1.8. Armed Conflict

A second major factor in the displacement of people and the creation of refugees has been armed conflict in Africa, which is thought to account for 30% of all refugees globally. A total of 18 million people are a cause for concern, primarily because of conflict in the Central African Republic (460,000 people have been displaced into neighbouring countries and 411,000 have been internally displaced), Southern Sudan (1.9 million people internally; 630,000 people in Uganda;

338,800 people in Ethiopia; 297,168 people in Sudan; 88,391 people in Kenya; 66,672 people in the Democratic Republic of the Congo, and 4,915 people in the Central African Republic), Burundi (409,000 people), Nigeria Mali (140,000 in neighbouring countries and 37,000 domestically displaced), Somalia (1.5 million internally displaced and 1 million in neighbouring countries), and Sudan (2.7 million internally displaced and 200,000 in neighbouring countries) (UNHCR, 2016]). In addition to internal displacement in Nigeria, there have been internal displacements in Cameroon (192,900), the Lake Region of Chad (82,260), and Niger (184,230). At the end of 2016, there were also 715,000 stateless persons living in Africa (UNHCR, 2017a).

1.9. Xenophobia

Xenophobia is an opposition to and hostility towards foreigners (Mcdonald & Jacobs, 2005). It is any form of fear involving a person or group that the person with the phobia perceives as being distinct from them. (Anon, 2013). This is clearly present within South Africa's population groups. Such xenophobia in South Africa has resulted in catastrophes that have severely damaged property, businesses, and ways of life. It is evident that early intervention is necessary before the xenophobic crisis reaches disaster levels as a result of the fact that many victims received assistance with transportation back to their home countries (Lawyers for Human Rights, 2015). However, South Africa has created adaptable and quick supply chains for humanitarian aid to support the phase of responding to xenophobic attacks. While it is important to closely monitor how swiftly and effectively humanitarian groups can respond to xenophobic humanitarian disasters, they tend to focus on saving lives, providing food and shelter to people who have lost their homes, and providing victims with essential health treatment (Schwarz & Kessler, 2010).

However, the biggest xenophobic attacks in South African history occurred in 2008, resulting in 62 fatalities and the expulsion of 35,000 people (Steinberg, 2008). Unfortunately, there is no assurance that similar eruptions won't occur again in the future. In conclusion, xenophobia constantly creates a risk that it may lead to humanitarian catastrophes in South Africa.

By dealing with some of the reasons for xenophobia, it is possible to address the remedies to humanitarian catastrophes caused by xenophobia. The primary ones are: the inability of the government to uphold law and order and to combat violent crimes (Cronje, 2008); foreign nationals accepting poverty-level wages; the failure of South Africa's foreign policy to condemn election fraud and dictatorship in other African countries leading to 'economic refugees'; corruption in immigration leading to fake work and residency permits; porous borders; the perception that foreigners are gaining access to South African women and jobs at the expense of locals (Mnyaka, 2009); and poor service delivery by all levels of government (Cronje, 2008).

That so, some people disagree with the claim that immigrants steal American employment. For instance, Nkosi (2010) claimed that some foreigners are well educated and skilled, but Steinberg (2010) said that some foreigners are simply grabbing employment rather than filling up gaps in the country. As an illustration, it is reported that due to a lack of teachers with these skills, more than 600 teachers were recruited from Zimbabwe to teach mathematics, science, and technology courses in the province of Limpopo.

1.10. Natural Disasters

Humanitarian unrest can also result from wildfires. Africa has numerous areas that are prone to drought, and wildfires have forced many people to flee their homes while also destroying their possessions. In South Africa, in particular, wildfires are now a major issue. Unchecked fires are damaging homes, pastures, farms, land, soil, forests, animal life, and shrub fields in addition to endangering human lives, health, and the environment. Additionally, wildfires use a significant amount of water, ruin livelihoods, raise insurance rates, endanger some species, and slow down economic growth. The dry summer and winter months are when the fires happen.

The primary culprits include abandoned campfires, the 'imbawula' heating stoves, which are most commonly seen in remote villages, lightning, fire debris, cigarette stumps, and fireworks (Forsyth et al., 2010). With a fire in the Table Mountain region affecting 500 people and necessitating the treatment of 52 elderly people for smoke inhalation, wildfires have also resulted in the loss of lives and the evacuation of properties. Six helicopters and two planes were required to put out the fire, which also destroyed or damaged a hotel lodge, homes, old wine vineyards, and offices. In June 2017, the Western Cape saw the biggest wildfire disaster in South Africa, which was primarily brought on by lightning. A total of nine people died, over 1,000 homes were destroyed, and 10,000 more were forced to flee their homes (Wild Fire Today, 2017).

1.11. Flooding

In general, the Emergency Events Database shows that 43% of the recorded catastrophes between 1994 and 2013 – which affected around 2.5 billion people – were caused by flooding. In addition to causing deaths, injuries, water contamination, property destruction, and a disruption in electricity supply, floods also leave 4 million people in Madagascar without enough food due to the locust swarms that follow them. Floods destroyed Morocco in 2014, while Malawi saw its worst floods in 50 years in 2015, with around 300 fatalities, 230,000 displaced residents, and 638,000 people affected. Flooding in Ethiopia followed the country's worst drought in decades, destroying whatever crops that had survived.

1.12. Climate Change

Climate variability and climate change worsen the situation in such cases making logistical operations extremely challenging. In some cases, helicopters and airfreight become the only viable rescue methods. In early 2017, Cyclone 'Dineo' brought torrential rains to South Africa with the subsequent floods causing damage to both property and the environment as well as 10.2 million people in need of food aid. Similar events in 2017 have severely impacted Madagascar and Sierra Leone (*The Guardian*, 2017).

1.13. Disasters and Sustainable Development in Africa

The African Ministerial Statement to the World Summit on Sustainable Development emphasised that the continent's efforts to achieve sustainable development are seriously hampered by the rising frequency of natural disasters in Africa (UNEP, 2001, para. 16). Africa's inability to foresee, monitor, manage, and prevent natural calamities makes this situation worse. Therefore, it is very concerning how prepared the continent is for disasters (Marjanovic & Nimpuno, 2003).

The difficulties include mismanagement of government-controlled reserves, slow NGO accreditation, economic decline and low recipient purchasing power, currency devaluation and inflation, high HIV infection rates, malnutrition, a shrinking labour force, unpredictable weather patterns, and dispersed populations. One of the biggest obstacles was specifically the worry that genetically modified grains will annihilate traditional crop kinds and endanger the viability of agriculture in the destination countries. It was thought that the long-term effects of importing genetically modified food into the local economy would have been worse than the short-term benefit of feeding hungry people in Southern Africa.

In order to lessen vulnerability and meet basic needs, Principle 8 of the Red Cross Code of Conduct emphasises the need to pay special attention to environmental issues in the design and management of humanitarian relief operations (IFRC, 2012). However, many humanitarian response operations still have a detrimental influence on the environment, and relief and recovery efforts can occasionally worsen the damage already done (UNEP, 2012). Unsustainable humanitarian efforts can lead to overexploitation of the environment and already-stressed natural resources.

Basic humanitarian operations can result in unsustainable practices such as the improper management and disposal of fuel, waste oil, tyres, chemicals and waste from operations based on logistics, or the procurement of goods made using unsustainable practices, all of which have the potential to reverse and overshadow the original intended good intentions. However, considering that the operation's goal is to meet urgent humanitarian needs, which is a matter of life or death, this component is frequently overlooked. This issue can be solved by creating more environmentally friendly supply chains and humanitarian operations that work to meet immediate needs without endangering the community's long-term social, economic, and environmental stability.

Other common sustainability issues are boreholes that run dry because of overpopulation and extensive deforestation, as well as displacement camps that were intended to provide temporary relief but instead last for years or decades (Encyclopedia of the Earth, 2009). In other words, failing to address risks, like the use of forests as a source of cooking wood, can undermine humanitarian efforts, leading to more casualties, displaced people, dependence on aid, and increased vulnerability. Although many NGOs and UN organisations are aware of this, there is still a significant study and action gap since the reality of humanitarian needs and operations takes precedence over these issues and hazards. On the other side, it is asserted (URD, 2008) that long-term humanitarian efforts enable a more seamless recovery. Therefore, it is obvious that research is needed to determine how humanitarian logistics and supply chain systems operations in Africa can be made to be environmentally sustainable. The knowledge obtained from this research also needs to be incorporated into research, teaching, and training curricula for humanitarian logisticians operations in Africa. The lessons could potentially have wider applications in nations and areas of the world that deal with comparable issues and circumstances.

1.14. Unpredictable Demand and Supply

Additionally, it is frequently necessary to conduct disaster relief activities in areas with unstable infrastructure, such as those with insufficient energy or poor transportation systems. Additionally, because the majority of natural disasters are unpredictable, so is the demand for commodities during these calamities. The capacity of logisticians to obtain, transport, and receive supplies at the location of a humanitarian relief operation determines how quickly aid arrives after a disaster (Thomas, 2003a, p. 4). Managing the humanitarian supply chain presents special difficulties since, in contrast to conventional supply chains, demand cannot be predicted (Long & Wood, 1995). It is challenging to determine supply and demand requirements in Africa due to the continent's weak political institutions and inadequate infrastructure, which also seriously complicate the fundamental requirement for flexibility in distribution (Buatsi et al., 2009; Scholten et al., 2010).

1.15. Efficiency of Disaster Response

The issue of how the international community responds to the difficulties brought on by natural disasters (e.g. floods, hurricanes, earthquakes, etc.) is raised by Ertem et al. (2010, p. 203). They noticed that NGOs, local governments, and the UN do not carry out disaster relief activities in a standard, effective manner that can overcome all disaster-related repercussions. Vital supplies (such as food, water, tents, clothing, medication, etc.) are typically not easily available to natural disaster victims in the aftermath.

Effective resource allocation, which is 'the primary purpose of disaster-relief organizations and NGOs during disaster-relief operations', can overcome this incapacity to send the resources to the catastrophe location in the right quantity and at the right time, according to Medina-Borja et al. (2007).

However, the speed with which emergencies are declared, the speed of responding to appeals, the calibre of assessments by national and international relief organisations, inefficiencies in transportation and procurement, and the degree of political interference are all matters of concern that were, for instance, all encountered during the 2007 floods in Northern Ghana (Buatsi et al., 2009).

1.16. The Need to Avoid Fixed and Irrelevant Logistics Networks

Traditional donors' food gifts meant for Africa have been rejected by several NGOs. This is due to the fact that donations frequently support and legitimise the subsidisation of the agricultural sector in the donor country, as well as the underutilisation of the donor's logistics networks and, in some cases, the sale of the food by NGOs and recipients at the expense of the sustainable food production in the recipient countries. The fixed logistics networks frequently fail to take into account the effects of food donations on local surplus food producers in neighbouring areas and nations. For instance, even though Malawi had abundant maize supplies, food assistance in Zimbabwe was dependent on the USA providing maize meal through established transportation networks. Over time, a series of additional catastrophes and donations may begin to harm the receiving economy rather than boost it. Donations thus have the potential to undermine local production volumes and capacity if they are not properly managed.

Some of Africa's natural calamities can be dealt with locally and nationally by using vendors who are closer to the area of need. To increase local capacity to respond to local emergencies and disasters, local production should be encouraged and supported by supply chains for disaster relief. Therefore, certain African economies may be usually better off without any food donations. This is because prices may increase to an extremely high level if dependency syndrome and donor fatigue develop.

Given the aforementioned difficulties, it is obvious that in order to meet the requirements of individuals who are affected, humanitarian logisticians need to pay close attention to a number of critical success elements. While it is acknowledged that there is a conflict between corporate-driven economic activity and the majority of African nations, it is suggested that the latter can benefit from the former (Nyaguthie, 2008).

For instance, Pettit and Beresford (2009) identified the following as areas where the know-how of the 'for profit' sector could be utilised: inventory management, transport and capacity planning, information management and technology utilisation, human resource management, continuous improvement and collaboration, and supply chain strategy. The importance of gender in humanitarian logistics operations in Africa, where Oxfam's experiences show that women perform better in humanitarian development initiatives, might be included to this list (Nyaguthie, 2008).

Given proper consideration, Richey (2009, p. 619) recommends that supply chain disaster and crisis preparedness and recovery be 'theoretically supported in combination of four mature theoretical perspectives': the resource-based view of the firm, communication theory, competing values theory, and relationship management theory. This will help us better understand how the operational efficiency of humanitarian supply networks may be increased.

This strategy is consistent with recent discussions in supply chain disaster and crisis management (and related supply chain strategy and logistics operations), where an emphasis is placed on factors that will help supply chain managers and researchers develop plans to get people out of harm's way and deliver aid to the impacted areas, such as agility (Oloruntoba & Gray, 2006), risk management/insurance issues (Kleidt et al., 2009), and humanitarian issues (Perry, 2007).

An additional important issue – language – that affects the majority of humanitarian logistics operations in Africa may be added to this extensive list. This reflects the fact that the majority of nations also speak other native tongues, such as French in Francophone Africa, Portuguese in the former Portuguese colonies, and English in the former English colonies (Nyaguthie, 2008).

1.17. Disaster Risk Management and Contingency Planning in Africa

Several nations have formed public institutions that work with international development and relief organisations to engage in disaster management efforts in response to the difficulties posed by catastrophes on the African continent. Depending on the country, institutional involvement might involve national governments as well as regional, provincial, state, district, and urban authorities. The Disaster Management Act 57 of 2002 of the Ekurhuleni Metropolitan Council in South Africa, for instance, describes disaster management as a continuous and integrated multi-sectoral, multi-disciplinary process of planning and putting into action measures targeted at: catastrophe preparedness, mitigation of disaster severity, and prevention or reduction of disaster risk are the top three priorities. Additionally, there is a definite need for (a) a quick and efficient reaction to disasters; (b) preparation and mapping of nations to aid in assessing the effects of catastrophes following flooding, volcanoes, earthquakes, or droughts; and (c) post-disaster recovery and rehabilitation. For instance, Ghana, which has formed a National Platform for Disaster Risk Reduction, employs similar strategies.

In order to prevent, reduce, plan for, respond to, and recover from the effects of all disasters, there are programmes and methods for disaster management in Africa. However, inadequate disaster preparedness through well-developed contingency plans, as well as limited response capability among governments and humanitarian groups in the area, frequently impede catastrophe response. According to Chatora (2005), some of the deficiencies found in disaster management include poor contingency planning and inadequate preparedness measures. Contingency plans must be created for each risk or potential disaster in order to respond to any crisis effectively. In fact, the importance of contingency planning in disaster management cannot be understated.

Contingency planning, among other things, facilitates the transition from 'a culture of reaction when disasters have happened, to a more preparedness culture', increases humanitarian accountability by preparing for, mitigating, and responding to disasters through agreed benchmarks, and promotes the creation and testing of new technologies. Without sufficient contingency planning, disaster management is not systematic, can be expensive, and may cause avoidable deaths as well as duplication of efforts and resource waste (UNHCR, 2011).

As a continual process, contingency planning necessitates ongoing assessment of the plan as circumstances change. Lessons were thus drawn from the Cyclone 'Eline' of 2000 in Southern Africa, which showed a lack of readiness and inadequate contingency preparation. In contrast, when Cyclone 'Favio' hit Mozambique in 2007, the ensuing flooding was quite severe, especially in the province of Inhambane, which was already experiencing significant floods. However, compared to 2000, the damage was low because of contingency preparation, early warning systems, and enhanced readiness capability.

The Disaster Management Authority of Mozambique had established flood and cholera contingency plans that could be triggered quickly in cooperation with other government ministries, UN organisations, the Red Cross, NGOs, and foreign humanitarian organisations. Pre-disaster human resource deployment to support operations in housing areas where displaced people were housed was one of them. Others included pre-positioning of stocks, having clearly defined roles and responsibilities, sharing information on available resources and gaps, and having pre-positioned stocks. This led to a rapid, coordinated response to disasters through the UN's cluster approach.

1.18. Analysis and Review

It is advised that a more thorough analysis of the distribution systems in the Developing World, with an emphasis on future transportation requirements, be carried out. Collaboration with other participants in the sector is also favoured. Donor organisations are also advised to help with road repair in remote places if governments are unable to do so.

The majority of Developing World nations lack reliable internal transportation and power systems. Due to the challenging economic climate, maintenance has been neglected for a number of years. Poorly surfaced roads with many potholes connect the major urban and industrial centres and cities, which slows down distribution operations and damages delivery trucks, leading to unforeseen delays and supply chain disruptions. It can also be a concern because the majority of the police officers on the streets are corrupt.

Governments in developing nations are urged to set up a clear-cut, long-lasting system for estimating and quantifying national commodity needs. Accurate consumption-based forecasts will only be possible if vital logistics information on the supplies given to victims is regularly gathered and reported. In order to provide a fuller view of the overall natural requirements, multiyear forecasting should also be carried out and recoded regularly to guarantee that assumptions made during the forecast are replaced with actual occurrences on the ground.

1.19. Procurement

Donor organisations handle the majority of the procurement, which is typically done without coordination and with a significant risk of duplication. The central coordination of procurement through information sharing between various NGOs, the government, and donor organisations is crucial. Information sharing should be encouraged to achieve this. They should be able to make significant purchases to take advantage of cheaper pricing as a result of growing their capacity, and they should be able to negotiate framework agreements with suppliers to control delivery in accordance with their requirements. Commodity procurement should always be integrated into the pipeline with other operational elements of the logistics system, such as forecasting and quantification, inventory control, and determining stock status. It has been observed that, for the most part, there is minimal direct correlation between the supply pipeline and the procurement actions, forecasting, and quantification. Procurement is mostly driven by the availability of funds; hence, more funds should be made available, such that more people can be assisted.

The majority of humanitarian aid organisations' present supply chain and logistical systems have a number of shortcomings, including: data must be typed into numerous spreadsheets and written out on numerous forms. Due to the difficulty and near impossibility of budget monitoring, monies may be misused, funds are not used as donors intended, procurement procedures are difficult to enforce, and integrity is lacking. Spreadsheets are used to manually track and trace shipments. Because reports are manually generated and there is no centralised database of past prices paid, transit times, or amounts received or purchased, little reporting and performance monitoring is done, other than informing donors of the number of supplies for a certain operation that were delivered. By boosting the efficacy of people and processes and establishing visibility into the materials pipeline, flexible technology solutions will enhance responsiveness (Thomas & Kopczak, 2005).

The following issues that the surveyed organisations face significantly limit their capacity to execute and function completely and effectively: government payments that be late, lower wages, certain donors' lack of dedication, stock shortages brought up by poor road conditions and weather, NGOs are discouraged by government engagement and regulation, and there is generally a large demand for therapy, which can be overwhelming.

It's also advised to establish a network for research, instruction, and education. It can launch and/or support educational initiatives in humanitarian logistics in the nations, producing a range of skills and credentials.

A centre for developing nations' humanitarian logistics and supply chains is thus suggested. The creation of a network for humanitarian logistics and supply chain actors from business, government, and academia is necessary to develop specialised solutions for humanitarian logistics. The investigation and focus can be on studying and modifying commercial and military logistics strategies and systems, as well as developing systems that react quickly and flexibly to changing and pressing needs and identifying gaps for taking advantage of synergies (Mbohwa 2008).

1.20. Concluding Remarks on Research Work on Humanitarian Logistics

Politics in the developed world can be easily regulated by law and is rather transparent. It is evident that the Developing World is politicising aid. Foreign donors face a challenging operating environment where well-intended aid appears to have unintentionally strengthened the ruling parties that frequently disrupt the supply chain and are also attempting to control it for their own benefits while unintentionally weakening the opposition forces. Therefore, politics must be eliminated from donor aid and donor agencies' operations for any organisation that wants to have a successful and even supply chain.

Politics in the developed world can be easily regulated by law and is rather transparent. It is evident that the Developing World is politicising aid. Foreign donors face a challenging operating environment where well-intended aid appears to have unwittingly strengthened the ruling parties that frequently disrupt the supply chain and are also attempting to dominate it for their own benefits while accidentally weakening the opposition forces. Therefore, politics must be eliminated from donor aid and donor agencies' operations for any organisation that wants to have a successful and even supply chain.

1.21. References

Buatsi, P., Oduro, F. T., Annan, J., Asamoah, D., & Boso, R. (2009). *Needs assessment in the delivery of relief to the 2007 Ghana flood disaster victims.* Proceedings of the 2nd Cardiff/Cranfield Humanitarian Logistics Initiative (CCHLI) international humanitarian logistic symposium, March 26, 2009, Sudbury House Hotel, Faringdon, Oxfordshire, UK.

Chatora, G. (2005). *A critical evaluation of the regional disaster response training programme of the International Federation of Red Cross and Red Crescent Societies in Southern Africa (2000–2004).* Zimbabwe Open University.

Clark, A., & Culkin, B. (2007). *A network transshipment model for planning humanitarian relief operations after a natural disaster.* Presented at EURO XXII – 22nd European conference on operational research, July 8, 2007 – July 11, 2007, Prague.

Cronje, F. (2008). Xenophobia: Nine causes of the current crises-NEWS and ANALYSIS.... Retrieved September 29, 2017, from http://www.politicsweb.co.za/news-and.../xeno-phobia-nine causes-of-the-current crises

Encyclopedia of the Earth. (2009). *Virunga National Park, Democratic Republic of Congo.* Retrieved November 11, 2013, from www.eoearth.org/article/Virunga_National_Park_Democratic_Republic_of_Congo

Ertem, M. A., Buyurgan, N., & Rossetti, M. D. (2010). Multiple-buyer procurement auctions framework for humanitarian supply chain management. *International Journal of Physical Distribution and Logistics Management, 40*(3), 202–227.

Forsyth, G. G., Kruger, F., & Le Maitre, D. C. (2010). National veldfire risk assessment: Analysis of exposure of social, economic and environmental assets to veldfire hazards in South Africa. Retrieved October 6, 2017, from https://www.westerncape.gov.za/assets/departments/local-government/Fire_Brigade_Services/For_the_fire_service/veldfire_risk_report_v11_0.pdf

IFRC. (2012). *Code of conduct for the International Red Cross and Red Crescent Movement and NGOs in disaster relief.* Retrieved November 11, 2012, from www.ifrc.org/Docs/idrl/I259EN.pdf

IPCC. (2012). *Managing the risks of extreme events and disasters to advance climate change adaptation: Special report of the Intergovernmental Panel on Climate Change.* Cambridge University Press. Retrieved December 2, 2013, from www.ipcc.ch/pdf/special-reports/srex/SREX_Full_Report.pdf

Kleidt, B., Schiereck, D., & Sigl-Grueb, C. (2009). Rationality at the eve of destruction: Insurance stocks and huge catastrophic events. *Journal of Business Valuation and Economic Loss Analysis, 4*(2), 1–25.

Kleindorfer, P. R., & Van Wassenhove, L. N. (2004). Managing risk in global supply chains in strategies for building successful global businesses. In H. Gatignon & J. R. Kimberley (Eds.), *The INSEAD-Wharton Alliance on Globalizing* (Chapter 12, pp. 288–305). Cambridge University Press.

Lawyers for Human Rights. (2015). *A new apartheid: South Africa's struggle with immigration.* Retrieved September 4, 2017, from http://www.lhr.org.za/news/2015/new-apartheid-south-africas-struggle-immigration

Long, D. C., & Wood, D. F. (1995). The logistics of famine relief. *Journal of Business Logistics, 16*(1), 213–229.

Marjanovic, P., & Nimpuno, K. (2003). Living with risk: Toward effective disaster management training in Africa. In A. Kreimer, M. Arnold, & A. Carlin (Eds.), *Building safer cities: The future of disaster risk.* (pp. 197–210) The World Bank. Retrieved December 7, 2013, from www.bvsde.paho.org/bvsacd/cd46/cap14-living.pdf

Mbohwa, C. (2008, May 5–9). *Identifying challenges and collaboration areas in humanitarian logistics: A Southern African perspective.* Proceedings of the conference on humanitarian logistics – Networks for Africa, Rockefeller Foundation, Bellagio Study and Conference Center, Bellagio, Lake Como, Italy.

Mcdonald, D. A., & Jacobs, S. (2005). (Re) writing xenophobia: Understanding press coverage of cross-border migration in Southern Africa. *Journal of Contemporary African Studies, 23*(3), 295–323.

Medina-Borja, A., Pasupathy, K. S., & Triantis, K. (2007). Large-scale data envelopment analysis (DEA) implementation: A strategic performance management approach. *Journal of the Operational Research Society, 58,* 1084–1098.

Mnyaka, M. M. N. (2009). *Xenophobia as a response to foreigners in post-apartheid South Africa and post-exilic Israel: A comparative critique in the light of the gospel and Ubuntu ethical principles* [Doctoral thesis]. Retrieved October 8, 2017, from, http://uir.unisa.ac.za/handle/10500/1176

Nkosi, A. (2010). *Zimbabwean teachers to fill our gaps.*

Nyaguthie, A. (2008, May 5–9). *Oxfam-GB – The important role of humanitarian logistics.* Proceedings of the conference on humanitarian logistics – Networks for Africa, Rockefeller Foundation, Bellagio Study and Conference Center, Bellagio, Lake Como, Italy.

Oloruntoba, R., & Gray, R. (2006). Humanitarian aid: An agile supply chain?, *Supply Chain Management: An International Journal, 11*(2), 115–120.

Perry, M. (2007). Natural disaster management planning: a study of logistics managers responding to the tsunami. *International Journal of Physical Distribution & Logistics Management, 37*(5), 409–433.

Pettit, S. J., & Beresford, A. K. C. (2009). Critical success factors in the context of humanitarian aid supply chains. *International Journal of Physical Distribution & Logistics Management, 39*(6), 450–468.

Qiang, Q., Nagurney, A., & Dong, J. (2008). Modeling of Supply Chain Risk under Disruptions with Performance Measurement and Robustness Analysis. In T. Wu, J. Blackhurst (Eds.), *Managing Supply Chain Risk And Vulnerability: Tools And Methods For Supply Chain Decision Makers.* Springer.

Richey, R. G. (2009). The supply chain crisis and disaster pyramid. A theoretical framework for understanding preparedness and recovery. *International Journal of Physical, Distribution & Logistics Management, 39*(7), 619–628.

Scholten, K., Sharkey-Scott, P., & Fynes, B. (2010). (Le)agility in humanitarian aid (NGO) supply chains. *International Journal of Physical Distribution and Logistics Management, 40*(8–9), 623–635.

Schwarz, J., & Kessler, M. (2010). Humanitarian logistics – TU Berlin (Logistik). Retrieved August 29, 2017, from http://www.logistik.tu-berlin.de/fileadmin/fg2/2010-10-27_vortrag_kessler_Schwarz.pdf

South Africa. (2002). *Disaster Management Act 57 of 2002.* Government Gazette. Retrieved December 7, 2013, from www.info.gov.za/view/DownloadFileAction?id=68094

Steinberg, J. (2008). *South Africa's xenophobic eruption* (ISS Papers, No. 169). Pretoria Institute for Security Studies. Retrieved October 8, 2017, from https://www.files.ethz.ch/isn/98954/PAPER169.pdf

Steinberg, J. (2010). Mother City offers little in way of succour to foreigners. *Sunday Times,* 7 November.

The Guardian. (2017). *Natural disasters and extreme weather.* Retrieved September 28, 2017, from https://www.theguardian.com/world/natural-disasters±africa

Thomas, A. (2003a). Why logistics? *Forced Migration, 18,* 4.

Thomas, A. (2003b). *Humanitarian logistics: Enabling disaster response.* The Fritz Institute.

Thomas, A., & Kopczak, L. (2005). *From logistics to supply chain management: The path forward in the humanitarian sector* (pp. 1–15) [Technical Report]. Fritz Institute, San Francisco, CA, USA.

Thompson, P. M. (2008). *Supply chain analytics for humanitarian logistics transformation.* Proceedings of the conference on humanitarian logistics: Network for Africa, Rockefeller Foundation, Bellagio Study and Conference Center, Bellagio, Lake Como, Italy.

Tomasini, R., Van Wassenhove, L. N. (2005). Managing information in humanitarian crisis: UNJLC Website. INSEAD Case 04/2005-5278.

UNDP. (2013). *Human development report 2013 – The rise of the south: Human progress in a diverse world.* United Nations Development Programme. Retrieved September 29, 2017, from, www.undp.org/content/dam/undp/library/corporate/HDR/2013GlobalHDR/English/HDR2013%20Report%20English.pdf

UNEP. (2001). *African ministerial statement to the world summit on sustainable development.* Retrieved December 6, 2013, from, www.unep.org/roa/docs/pdf/African%20ministerial%20statement_english_.pdf

UNEP. (2012). *Sudan post-conflict environmental assessment.* UNEP. Retrieved November 11, 2013, from, www.unep.org/sudan/

UNHCR. (2011). *Contingency planning.* Retrieved December 6, 2013, from, http://epdfiles.engr.wisc.edu/dmcweb/EP01ContingencyPlanning.pdf

UNHCR. (2016). *Africa regional summary.* Retrieved from https://www.unhcr.org/afr/publications/%20fundraising/593e4bf27/unhcr-global-report-2016-africa-regional-summary.html

UNHCR. (2017a). *Africa.* Retrieved September 28, 2017, from, http://www.unhcr.org/africa.html

UNHCR. (2017b). *Regional summaries: Africa.* http://www.unhcr.org/afr/publications/fundraising/593e4bf27/unhcr-global-report-2016-africa-regional-summary.html

UNISDR. (2015). *The human cost of natural disasters: A global perspective.* https://reliefweb.int/report/world/human-cost-natural-disasters-2015-global-perspective

URD. (2008). *Humanitarian aid on the move.* Retrieved November 11, 2013, from, www.urd.org/IMG/pdf/URD_newsletter1_p_UK.pdf

USAID. (2012). *Working in crises and conflict.* Retrieved September 30, 2013, from, www.usaid.gov/what-we-do/working-crises-and-conflict

Van Wassenhove, L. N. (2006). Blacket memorial lecture. Humanitarian aid logistics: Supply chain management in high gear. *Journal of Operational Research Society, 57*(5), 475–489.

WFF. (2016). *Water facts and futures. Rethinking South Africa's water futures.* Retrieved August 29, 2017, from http://awsassets.wwf.org.za/downloads/wwf009_water-factsandfutures_report_web__lowres_.pdf

Wild Fire Today. (2017). *Wild fire South Africa.* Retrieved October 8, 2017, from http://wildfiretoday.com/tag/south-africa/

Chapter 2

Frameworks Supporting Humanitarian Logistics

2.1. Introduction

In order to address the variety of issues posed by disasters across the continent, African governments are working cooperatively to improve the efficacy and efficiency of institutional policies. Consequently, an Africa Regional Strategy for Disaster Risk Reduction has been established by the African Union (AU) under its New Partnership for Africa's Development. The AU has noted that the majority of the factors influencing disaster vulnerability in Africa are results of or pressures on development, and that most African nations have not yet incorporated disaster management into their national development frameworks (Buatsi et al., 2009).

Together with development partners, international relief and development organisations such as World Vision International, Action Aid, Care International, Oxfam, and ADRA (among others) are addressing the problems by developing and implementing various interventions across the continent. However, the aforementioned measures aimed at reducing disaster risk and the variety of difficulties connected with these efforts have ramifications for humanitarian logistics and supply chain management. This is particularly true in Africa due to the uncertainties surrounding the determination of demand and supply for humanitarian relief, which typically leans more towards emergencies than development (Buatsi et al., 2009).

The discipline of humanitarian logistics needs to create new theories to better understand the logistics requirements at various stages of a crisis and how to address them. This chapter will analyse three characteristics found in logistics and organisational theories and how they relate to three separate humanitarian logistics cases. The goal is to provide a framework that may be applied to future research.

2.2. Building Theory of Human Supply Chain (HSC) Policy

Researchers who study humanitarian logistics work to advance the understanding of how logistics may strengthen communities and improve their capacity to

Supply Networks in Developing Countries:
Sustainable and Humanitarian Logistics in Growing Consumer Markets, 19–29
Copyright © 2023 by Tatenda Talent Chingono and Charles Mbohwa
Published under exclusive licence by Emerald Publishing Limited
doi:10.1108/978-1-80117-194-620231002

respond to disasters. What coordination mechanisms, organisational structures, and processes can be identified in the many aspects of humanitarian relief, and how these connect to theories and models used in the field of logistics, are some of the areas that need to be researched. As was determined following the 2004 tsunami tragedy and in earlier logistics studies (Van Wassenhove, 2006), readiness and responsiveness go hand in hand. As a result, attention is focussed on how permanent networks interact with temporary networks during the planning and preparation phases and with the return to permanent logistical solutions during the recovery phase.

(1) *Permanent and temporary networks* – connections between the ongoing structures and networks of humanitarian players and the temporary networks formed when a crisis strikes.
(2) *Vertical and horizontal coordination* – difficulties in coordinating horizontally among actors within an area of operations due to the presence of numerous organisations of various types in big crises, as well as difficulties in coordinating vertically when supply chains stretch into uncharted areas.
(3) *Centralised and de-centralised structures* – to improve the capacity to respond to disasters, decisions need to be made on what activities and resources should be performed at decentralised locations and what ones should be preserved in a central location (Jahre et al., 2009).

2.3. Humanitarian Logistics Frameworks and Policy

The setting in which humanitarian organisations work presents a complex range of difficulties, including unpredictable demand (in terms of timing, location, type, and size), sudden occurrences of large demands with short lead times for various supplies, the significance of on-time deliveries, and a lack of resources (material, human, technology, and financial). Depending on what is deemed transportation expenditures, logistics can account for up to 80% of a programme budget for these organisations or up to 40% of operating costs, compared to 15% for logistic activities in the commercial sector (Jahre et al., 2009). Since many humanitarian groups may participate in an emergency response and share the same overarching objectives of assisting the afflicted population, there is potential for them to coordinate their efforts in order to provide a more effective response. The problem of cooperation in humanitarian logistics has been extensively studied, and one method of coordination is the consolidation of commodities. Through a survey of pertinent publications that results in the establishment of a theoretical framework, the goal of this study is to develop a theoretical framework to better understand the motivations and barriers to material consolidation in humanitarian logistics. Frameworks offer the possibility to simplify a representation of reality and help in the elaboration of theories. Frameworks not only address topics in the literature but also help present the different relevant issues at hand and how they interact with each other. An overall picture of the incentives and obstacles can lead to more empirical field work and to a better understanding of the relevant literature for humanitarian logistics. This can be done by offering new ways of interpreting data as well as defining research problems. Frameworks and policies offer practitioners a better understanding of the general considerations behind the management of consolidation materials and how they can address them depending on their own context. Frameworks apply to a specific instance of coordination in context of humanitarian logistics.

Disaster relief and management is identified as one setting that significantly affects supply chain design decision and features. Frameworks and policies focus on a conceptual description which identifies relevant concepts and propositions relative to consolidation in humanitarian logistics. This answers the call for more theory building according to the three dimensions relevant to humanitarian logistics, that is, network, coordination, and structure, as suggested by Jahre et al. (2009). Consolidation essentially consists of the management of a centralised coordination structure (Kovács & Spens, 2007).

2.4. Humanitarian Logistics Coordination and Frameworks

Consolidation of materials is one of the possibilities that are available to organisations to gain economies of scale and other performance benefits in their supply chain activities. Consolidation is a topic that is generally understood in the business literature as combining certain activities or materials that have common attributes to improve the overall performance of firms. Consolidation can range from market consolidation in which companies combine their assets and activities, to information technology systems where companies integrate different software packages (Grosswiele et al., 2013). For the purpose of this study, consolidation is viewed in the context of materials management where materials are regrouped together physically through management activities. This type of consolidation consists of inventory, transportation, and purchasing activity. In this context, specific definitions of consolidation exist. Inventory consolidation is stocking items at a single facility which satisfies all demand (Wanke & Saliby, 2009). Transportation consolidation is the dispatch of small amounts of material in a single large more economic load. Purchasing consolidation occurs when purchases are regrouped to gain certain benefits. Even though consolidation is present in humanitarian operations, there is little to no literature regarding the practice of consolidation of goods in humanitarian logistics (Schulz & Blecken, 2010).

Cooperation and coordination are well discussed topics in humanitarian logistics literature, and consolidation can be considered a specific subtopic. Balick et al. (2010) discuss coordination in humanitarian logistics through the different coordination mechanisms that cover purchasing, warehousing, and transportation and put forward the critical role of coordination as well as the increased partnerships found in humanitarian logistics. Coordination is as important as funding issues, needs assessment and procurement, management of information, transportation infrastructure and network design, and standardisation of relief (Jahre et al., 2009).

Jahre et al. (2009) developed a theoretical framework for humanitarian logistics that include both vertical and horizontal coordination. The authors also investigate the challenges of vertical and horizontal cooperation in humanitarian clusters where limited resources force tradeoffs between intercluster and intracluster collaboration. Kovács and Spens (2007) highlighted the importance of coordination and collaboration between regional and extra-regional actors at different steps of the disaster phase. Most researchers point out that coordination takes place within a relational network under conditions of competition and confusion. Coordination and collaboration can also be significant for cost savings in humanitarian logistics but limited because of the competition for funding. Coordination can be facilitated through web-based systems, membership subscription, mechanisms to mitigate risk and cost allocation, easy to use sharing and information tools, and feedback mechanisms to facilitate learning as well as challenges for consolidation (large number and diversity of participants, urgency of relief and limited time for coordination, limited information sharing and communication, allocation of costs and benefits, and limited personnel dedicated to coordination; Jahre et al., 2009).

The challenges to collaboration are also reviewed in literature as the number and diversity of actors, donor expectations, competition, effects of the media, unpredictability, resource scarcity or oversupply, cost, determining and dividing gains, and lack of standardisation (Jahre et al., 2009).

Logistics and supply chain analytical frameworks are common in the business-oriented literature and address various topics such as integrated supply chains, build-to-order supply chains, and supply chain vulnerability. There are different frameworks in humanitarian logistics (Jahre et al., 2009; Kovács & Spens, 2007) and they use different levels of abstraction in how they develop the various concepts. Jahre et al. (2009) put forward a high abstraction model which identifies theory development possibilities through different dimensions (Jahre et al., 2009). These dimensions comprise types of structure (decentralised/centralised), coordination (vertical/horizontal), and network (permanent/temporary).

2.5. Multiplicity of Actors: The Critical Roles of Inter-agency Communication, Collaboration, and Coordination

Richey (2009) contends that relationship management theory can help us better understand collaboration in humanitarian logistics and supply chain management because there are typically multiple players involved in such situations. Governments, domestic non-governmental organisations (NGOs), international NGOs, military organisations, and United Nations (UN) relief organisations are among the diverse groups of actors that can be present in a disaster situation, according to Pettit and Beresford (2009). Accordingly, it is believed that the development of an effective supply chain depends on both the 'structural' and 'cultural' components of supply chains. While the prior discussion in this chapter clearly shows that there is some collaboration among the groups engaged in humanitarian aid initiatives in Africa, there is undoubtedly more work to be done. Particularly, integrating the efforts of international organisations,

NGOs, etc. with those of national and regional African organisations aid in better strategic planning and implementation in regard to humanitarian logistics and supply chain management.

Humanitarian crises like those that happened in Somalia, Kosovo, and Afghanistan are defined by multinational humanitarian and military efforts, according to Ford et al. (2002). These crises are complicated and pose a very difficult operational setting because they involve extremely delicate political, military, and humanitarian issues. Communication, collaboration, and coordination are essential for actors reacting to such a complex humanitarian catastrophe since they need one another to address the problem. During complicated humanitarian emergencies, technology can greatly aid information sharing between the various participants (Kovács & Tatham, 2009).

In a similar vein, a wide range of parties are involved in humanitarian assistance efforts in Africa, including governments and governmental agencies, the UN, people, military personnel, NGOs, businesses, and religious institutions (Scholten et al., 2010). These organisations work to better the lives of Africans by supplying necessities including water, food, clothing, housing, medical supplies, medical care, and fundamental human rights. Aid organisations, which are considered as the main actors through which governments channel aid that is intended to alleviate suffering caused by natural and man-made disasters, determine demand (Long & Wood, 1995). The biggest organisations are international players, but there are also several minor regional and national relief organisations (Thomas & Kopczak, 2005). The military, host, and neighbouring country governments, other NGOs, and logistics service providers are examples of other participants. In Africa, as in many (if not all) other parts of the world, this presents a significant challenge. The advantages of an inter-agency contingency planning outweigh the individual organisational benefits and allow for information and resource sharing, while minimising duplication and confusion among organisations.

2.6. Human Capacity Building for Disaster Risk Management in Africa

Humanitarian logistics in Africa has large, varied, and multidisciplinary training and capacity building needs. However, there aren't enough training facilities/units and there isn't enough capacity. According to Marjanovic and Nimpuno (2003), effective disaster management training and capacity building must be developed and implemented in Africa using a cooperative network approach. In order to address the long-term needs of the area, Africa must construct a solid and sustainable training and capacity-building programme.

2.7. Policies for Training in Disaster Management

A blend of formal training programmes in disaster management leading to undergraduate and postgraduate qualifications, with a focus on basics of disaster management from a practical point of view, is greatly needed. For public sector employees in some African countries, like those in the National Disaster

Management Organization, who also profit from training abroad, structured training programmes have been devised. While professional organisations like the Chartered Institute of Logistics and Transport have integrated courses in humanitarian logistics for professional certification in collaboration with Institutes of Management and Public Administration, representatives of international relief organisations, regularly undergo internal training both domestically and abroad according to Buatsi et al. (2009).

The Disaster Risk Management Training and Education Centre for Africa at the University of The Free State provides postgraduate instruction and training in the Republic of South Africa. The Disaster Management Institute of South Africa additionally provides training in disaster management. The Provincial Disaster Management Centre of the Western Cape began disaster management/integrated development plan (IDP) training, which was directed at municipal politicians and officials engaged in the field of disaster management, in response to the Disaster Management Act (No. 52 of 2002) and the Municipal Systems Act (No. 32 of 2000), which stipulate the inclusion of a disaster management plan into the municipality's IDP. The Disaster Management Act is being implemented throughout the province as part of a strategy that includes this capacity-building programme.

2.8. Policy and Framework Challenges of Humanitarian Logistics in Africa

The challenges of humanitarian logistics in Africa have been highlighted in the preceding discussions. The following is a summary of those challenges:

(A) *Inadequate resources and infrastructure*: Most of the continent of Africa has subpar infrastructure, which makes it difficult to respond quickly to calamities. To overcome this obstacle, third generation communication technology and the widespread usage of cellular phones have helped in fields like telemedicine, early warning systems, and better information and communication during disasters (Kovács et al., 2007).

(B) *Lack of effective institutional frameworks and policies*: While institutional frameworks and policies for disaster risk reduction do exist in many African countries, their efficacy is limited. As a result, African disaster risk management systems are now unable to sufficiently mitigate and manage disaster risks (African Union, 2004). Firefighters from South Africa, for instance, have helped those in Canada, Australia, and other nations outside of Africa, but there seems to be less emphasis on comparable intra-African partnerships (Kovács & Tatham, 2009).

(C) *Lack of standards and indicators*: Standards and indicators are lacking in Africa, which has yet to harmonise national policies and initiatives to support continental and regional operations. These are crucial for coordinated efforts to combat calamities. Africa must learn to respond more quickly than others do (Kovács et al., 2007).

(D) *Poor coordination*: Humanitarian operations in Africa suffer from a major lack of coordination, which can lead to incompatible plans and initiatives. For instance, after a recent xenophobic incident, neighbouring nations began repatriating their afflicted individuals while the South African government was putting up temporary shelters for victims (Kovàcs et al., 2007).

(E) *Poor collaboration*: When parties don't work together to share information, it frequently leads to wasted time and effort. The collaboration of humanitarian activities in Africa is hampered by a lack of coordination (Kovács et al., 2007).

(F) *Lack of needs assessment*: Following a disaster, determining what is needed is essential for effective relief efforts. Sadly, when international assistance organisations get on the scene after a tragedy, they typically undertake needs assessments due to the lack of knowledge in Africa. African governments claim that they do not have the manpower and or resources to carry out needs assessments and even feasibility studies (Kovács & Tatham, 2009).

(G) *Lack of appreciation of logistics and supply chain management*: Within NGOs and humanitarian relief organisations, there is a common lack of understanding of the contribution and, consequently, significance of the function of humanitarian logistics. This calls for greater training, particularly as new difficulties emerge. The current wildfire outbreak in South Africa's Western Cape serves as one such difficulty. Even though the country was suffering from a severe drought, greater disaster planning could have reduced the scope and impact of the disaster, particularly in Knysna. Africa is prepared to adopt supply chain management and logistics, but there aren't enough logisticians working there. This significantly impedes efforts to use supply chain management and humanitarian logistics principles to improve operational performance and cost effectiveness in humanitarian relief. Due to a severe lack of training in the field, this is made worse (Nyaguthie, 2008).

(H) *Governance*: According to Mbohwa (2008), transparency and accountability, the two main tenets of good governance, are areas where many organisations fall short. Many organisations lack efficient systems that ensure they consistently gain the trust of stakeholders in the areas of financial management, programme monitoring and evaluation, and managing overall programme performance. Usually, only a small number of other members participate in the control and management of the organisation's affairs by the founder or founders.

There are no strategic plans to help the organisation understand its goals and help it determine the resources it needs. The majority of strategic plans created are primarily for the benefit of donors and do not take into account the actual requirements of the community. A board is rarely effective at providing strategic leadership to ensure that resources are mobilised, and NGOs in many countries lack efficient governance structures (Perry, 2007). The purpose of boards is to direct and monitor an NGO's operations. Many boards, however, are unaware of their part in resource mobilisation. The existence and level of management and governance structures in NGOs have an impact on their capacity to mobilise funding. Frequently, NGOs lacked governance tools (Pettit & Beresford, 2009).

2.9. Benefits of Merging

Nonprofit organization (NPO) or non-profit organisation must merge as a group if they want to increase their chances of success with regard to finance and ongoing operations. The organisations will gain in terms of people resources, knowledge, favourable reputation, and programme strengthening according to Mbohwa (2008).

2.10. Humanitarian Policy in Response to Tougher Host Government Regulations

Government regulations can contribute to the professionalisation of logistics in one of two ways. First, this can be through the direct support and recognition of certain functions as professions. Second, governments can use regulations to push for positive change in specific industries, thereby initiating the development of certain skills and capabilities of the professionals therein. For example, the growing concerns about global warming have triggered regulations intended to reduce polluting logistics activities. In turn, organisations have responded through compliance and/or proactive adjustments before new regulatory implementation to ensure good logistics performance. These responses may require additional training to increase knowledge of the prevailing regulations and how to comply with them and, here, professional certification organisations can play a significant role (Pohlen, 2011).

Government regulations can also be used for political or economic reasons that result in negative consequences for timely and efficient processing, for example, trade restrictions, customs 5 procedures, and discriminatory regulations aimed at protectionism and taxation. In humanitarian operations, organisations increasingly depend on the host governments' permission to assist disaster victims, a largely political issue. Furthermore, the push for change in terms of economy and quality control has led to an increase in regulations affecting international procurement and donations by international health organizations (IHOs) (Kunz & Gold, 2017). Whatever the reasons for a host government's actions, logistics performance is highly dependent on the humanitarian logisticians' ability to comply with local and national government regulations. This hinges on the development of humanitarian logistics as a profession. The humanitarian identity and the professional identity do not always converge, and this can impose contradictory requirements on an individual. For example, some governments can use regulations to ensure the exclusion of disaster victims in desperate need of assistance, and import restrictions could expose beneficiaries to potentially harmful products. When individuals are confronted with such differences in their social identities, they make an effort, in defining the social self, to reconcile the competing implications. Members within the same occupational group can have differing interpretations of the same phenomenon, such as, in the case of humanitarian logisticians, import restrictions. Consequently, they can have different ways of reconciling the diverging identities and thus can have differing responses to that phenomenon (Grbic, 2010).

2.11. Conclusion

The immense scope of the function of humanitarian logistics within the African setting becomes obvious when considering the unpredictable nature of disasters and its accompanying demand and supply needs. It has been established that it is crucial to take into account the effectiveness and degree of success of humanitarian response and recovery activities by a variety of actors who exhibit varying degrees of coordination and cooperation. As a result, in the African context as well as elsewhere, it is crucial to identify critical success drivers and to anchor humanitarian supply network management in strong management theory. There are signs of change that will steadily increase the effectiveness of humanitarian supply networks, including institutional developments in and adoption of disaster risk management, including policy development, strategic planning, inter-agency communication, collaboration, and coordination, the adoption of a variety of technologies to facilitate hazard analysis, vulnerability assessment, contingency planning, reporting systems, and early warning systems.

Building up human capital at all levels in all facets of disaster management, such as supply chain management and humanitarian logistics, must be done in addition to these efforts. With three mini-cases in Southern Africa that concentrate on the hotspots, Zimbabwe, South Africa, and Botswana, the HIV/AIDS epidemic has been treated in some detail. These contribute to the body of information and the conversation around supply chains and humanitarian logistics for slow-onset disasters in Africa. The expanding role of third generation cellular networks, supported by broad band transmission systems and fibre optics technology, is an intriguing aspect. This technology is enabling better information flow, which in turn is improving early warning systems, communication, information dissemination and exchange, and recovery systems.

These viewpoints on logistics for humanitarian aid in Africa draw attention to the scale of the problem, but they also support the idea that as various levels of development are accomplished, management of supply networks for aid organisations in Africa will eventually become more efficient and effective. Above all, the issues raised should serve as a guide for the creation of research models of the continent's humanitarian supply networks, which would improve the effectiveness of the logisticians who work in this field for the various organisations that operate there.

2.12. References

African Union. (2004). Retrieved from https://www.undrr.org/publication/africa-regional-strategy-disaster-risk-reduction
Balick, B. et al., (2010). Coordination in humanitarian relief chains: Practices, challenges and opportunities. *International Journal of Production Economics, 126*(1), 22–34.
Buatsi, P., Oduro, F. T., Annan, J., Asamoah, D., & Boso, R. (2009). *Needs assessment in the delivery of relief to the 2007 Ghana flood disaster victims.* Proceedings of the 2nd Cardiff/Cranfield Humanitarian Logistics Initiative (CCHLI) international humanitarian logistic symposium, Sudbury House Hotel, Faringdon, Oxfordshire, UK.

Ford, T. D., Hogan, J. L., Perry M. W. (2002) *Communication during complex humanitarian emergencies: Using technology to bridge the gap.* Thesis. Naval Postgraduate School, Monterey, California. https://apps.dtic.mil/sti/pdfs/ADA407012.pdf.

Grbic, N. (2010). "Boundary work" as a concept for studying professionalization processes in the interpreting field. *Translation and Interpreting Studies, 5*(1), 109–123.

Grosswiele, L., Roeglinger, M., & Friedl, B. (2013). A Decision Framework for the Consolidation of Performance Measurement Systems. *Decision Support Systems, 54,* 1016–1029. 10.1016/j.dss.2012.10.027.

Jahre, M., Jensen, L. M., & Listou, T. (2009). Theory development in humanitarian logistics: A framework and three cases. *Management Research News, 32,* 1008–1023.

Long, D. C.., & Wood, D. F. (1995). The logistics of famine relief. *Journal of Business Logistics, 16*(1), 213–229.

Kovács, G., & Spens, K. M. (2007). Humanitarian logistics in disaster relief operations. *International Journal of Physical Distribution & Logistics Management, 37*(2), 99–114.

Kovács, G., Spens, K. M., & Buatsi, P. (2007). *Challenges of humanitarian logisticians in Africa.* Proceedings of the 1st Cardiff/Cranfield Humanitarian Logistics Initiative (CCHLI) international humanitarian logistic symposium, Sudbury House Hotel, Faringdon, Oxfordshire, UK.

Kovács, G., & Tatham, P. H. (2009). Responding to disruptions in the supply network – From dormant to action. *Journal of Business Logistics, 30*(2), 215–229.

Kunz, N., & Gold, S. (2017). Sustainable humanitarian supply chain management – exploring new theory. *International Journal of Logistics Research and Applications. 20,* 85–104. 10.1080/13675567.2015.1103845.

Marjanovic, P., & Nimpuno, K. (2003). Living with risk: Toward effective disaster management training in Africa. In A. Kreimer, M. Arnold, & A. Carlin (Eds.), *Building safer cities: The future of disaster risk* (pp. 197–210). The World Bank (Accessed 7 December 2013).

Mbohwa, C. (2008, May 5–9). *Identifying challenges and collaboration areas in humanitarian logistics: A Southern African perspective* [Conference proceedings]. Proceedings of the conference on humanitarian logistics – Networks for Africa Rockefeller Foundation Bellagio Study and Conference Center, Bellagio, Lake Como, Italy.

Nyaguthie, A. (2008, May 5–9). *Oxfam-GB – The important role of humanitarian logistics* [Conference proceedings]. Proceedings of the conference on humanitarian logistics – Networks for Africa, Rockefeller Foundation Bellagio Study and Conference Center, Italy.

Perry, M. (2007). Natural disaster management planning: A study of logistics managers responding to the tsunami. *International Journal of Physical Distribution & Logistics Management, 37*(5), 409–433.

Pettit, S. J., & Beresford, A. K. C. (2009). Critical success factors in the context of humanitarian aid supply chains. *International Journal of Physical Distribution & Logistics Management, 39*(6), 450–468.

Pohlen, T. L. (2011). Meeting the Challenge of Educating the Transportation and Logistics Professional: The American Society of Transportation and Logistics on the 50th Anniversary of *Transportation Journal. Transportation Journal, 50*(1): 84 -90. https://doi.org/10.5325/transportationj.50.1.0084

Richey, R. G. (2009). The supply chain crisis and disaster pyramid. A theoretical framework for understanding preparedness and recovery. *International Journal of Physical, Distribution & Logistics Management, 39*(7), 619–628.

Scholten, K., Sharkey Scott, P., & Fynes, B. (2010). (Le)agility in humanitarian aid (NGO) supply chains. *International Journal of Physical Distribution & Logistics Management, 40*(8/9), 623–635. https://doi.org/10.1108/09600031011079292

Schulz, S., & Blecken, A. (2010). Horizontal cooperation in disaster relief logistics: Benefits and impediments. *International Journal of Physical Distribution & Logistics Management, 40*, 636–656. 10.1108/09600031011079300.

Thomas, A., & Kopczak, L. (2005). *From logistics to supply chain management: The path forward in the humanitarian sector* (pp. 1–15) [Technical report]. Fritz Institute, San Francisco, CA, USA.

Van Wassenhove, L. N. (2006). Humanitarian aid logistics: Supply chain management at high gear. *Journal of the Operational Research Society, 57*, 475–489. Retrieved from https://www.tandfonline.com/doi/abs/10.1057/palgrave.jors.2602125

Wanke, P. F., & Saliby, E. (2009). Consolidation effects: Whether and how inventories should be pooled. *Transportation Research Part E: Logistics and Transportation Review, 45*(5), 678–692.

Chapter 3

Disasters in Selected Emerging Economies

3.1. Introduction

There have been a lot more documented disasters in Africa since the 1970s. Over the past 40 years, there have been over a thousand disasters in Sub-Saharan Africa. The possibility of disasters to progress puts many recent developments in jeopardy. As a result of climate change, extreme hydro-meteorological events, which make up Africa's disaster profile, are expected to occur more frequently and with greater severities. The region's disaster profile is closely tied to the vulnerability of Sub-Saharan Africa's economy and population, as well as to their frequently constrained capacities to deal with natural disasters.

According to the United Nations Office for Disaster Risk Reduction (UNDRR, 2020), floods frequently occur along the major river systems and in many urban areas, but droughts continue to damage the biggest number of people on the continent. The majority of disasters in Africa are hydro-meteorological in nature. Madagascar, Mozambique, and a few islands in the Indian Ocean are the main targets of cyclones. Along the Rift Valley, geological hazards that are less severe are more common. Africa's low-lying coastal regions are becoming more and more vulnerable to storm surges, coastal erosion, and sea-level rise. Climate change is expected to result in an increase in the severity and frequency of these extreme weather occurrences. The vulnerability of the people and economies of Sub-Saharan Africa, which is rendered worse by the area's insufficient coping mechanisms, has a significant impact on the region's disaster profile. Most African countries lack the funds necessary to invest in disaster risk. Disasters have a significant negative impact on the economy's performance and expansion. Poor, small island governments, and landlocked countries are particularly vulnerable to the financial effects of disasters. Many local and national distributed resource management (DRM) agencies still have limited capacity. Numerous regions rely heavily on rain-fed agriculture, which is extremely sensitive to climate change. Critical infrastructure of roads, telecoms, and dams often fall short of the fast increasing demand or are not constructed to risk-prone standards. The majority of Africa's economic resources are located in heavily populated urban regions close to river deltas or other bodies of water.

Supply Networks in Developing Countries:
Sustainable and Humanitarian Logistics in Growing Consumer Markets, 31–44
Copyright © 2023 by Tatenda Talent Chingono and Charles Mbohwa
Published under exclusive licence by Emerald Publishing Limited
doi:10.1108/978-1-80117-194-620231003

Many urban dwellers reside in unauthorised communities commonly found in locations that are vulnerable to disasters, such as floodplains or drainage basins.

3.2. AU Regional Strategy

(1) Enables sector-specific assessments of catastrophe risk and susceptibility and strengthens early warning and monitoring systems.
(2) Promotes DRM awareness and institutional and policy development executive summary.
(3) Makes investments to reduce risk and addresses underlying risk issues.
(4) Encourages the development of new finance tools for preparedness, emergency, and catastrophic risk.
(5) Boosts emergency preparedness and response and help after disasters.

The primary partners for its execution are the national governments, their national DRM organisations, and national platforms. The Africa DRM team launched risk and vulnerability assessments as its initial set of activities in order to put these goals into practice. At first, they discussed the effects on the economy, urban flooding, water resource management, food security during droughts, marine ecosystems, and capacity building programmes (UNDRR, 2020).

3.3. Sub-Saharan Africa's Disaster Profile

The danger of disaster is complex and continues to undergo rapid change in sub-Saharan African nations. According to the UNDRR (2020), over 157 million people were directly and indirectly impacted by disasters across 44 nations from 2008 to 2018, as shown in Figure 3.1; the majority of these were linked to natural hazards. Hydro-meteorological or climatological risks, primarily droughts, floods, storms, and cyclones, are what cause the majority of disasters in Africa. A total of 47,543 people died as a result of natural disasters between 2010 and 2018, 15,173 people died as a result of technologically related catastrophes, and 225,237 injuries have been connected to disaster events in the same 10 years. Of these, 14,376 injuries were brought on by technological risks, whereas 210,861 injuries were brought on by natural disasters according to the UNDRR (2020). Epidemics were the primary factor in the majority of fatalities from natural disasters (37,418 or 79%), landslides (6,468 or 14% of all floods), or floods (2,055 or 4%). Between 2008 and 2018, more than 100,000 people were harmed by technology risks, and 15,173 people passed away. Transport accidents (road, water, rail, and air) made up 81% of all disaster events involving technological hazards. Miscellaneous accidents (structural collapse, explosions, fires, and others) made up 12% of total occurrence, and industrial accidents (chemical spills, structural collapse, explosions, fire, gas leak, poisoning, radiation, and oil spills) made up 7%.

Nearly all of Sub-Saharan Africa's nations are susceptible to one or more natural dangers.

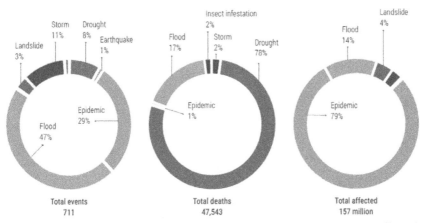

Fig. 3.1.   Summary of Impact by Natural Disaster Events and People Affected from 2008 to 2018. *Source*: Adapted from UNDRR (2020).

Large river basins like those in the Congo, Niger, Nile, and Zambezi typically experience flooding, but flash floods can occur anywhere where there has been an unusually heavy rainfall. In the Sahelian nations, the Horn of Africa, and Southern Africa, droughts are most common in semiarid and subhumid regions. In nations with mountainous terrain, high rainfall, soil erosion, and deforestation as a result of irresponsible land management, the risk of landslides is significant. Countries on the southeast coast of the Indian Ocean are affected by cyclones and tropical storms.

However, the way we perceive danger is rapidly changing. All risk analyses must take probability into consideration as well as account for uncertainty. Probabilistic risk assessment estimates probability and takes into account a wide range of potential outcomes, their likelihood, and any resulting effects. Probabilistic risk profiles for flood and drought were created for some sub-Saharan African nations in 2018 and 2019, as part of a programme called 'Building Disaster Resilience to Natural Hazards in Sub-Saharan African Regions, Countries and Communities' sponsored by the European Union. A variety of sectors committed to the Sendai goals, including housing, health and education, agriculture, productive assets, essential infrastructure, housing, services, and transportation, are anticipated to suffer financial losses as a result of this quantitative risk assessment. In order to refine the research' conclusions and create information that can be used to develop country-specific policy recommendations, datasets were incorporated.

Probabilistic risk assessments are tools for diagnosing risks; they give warnings of potential adverse events and their effects. The initial phase in cost-benefit assessments of investments and policies for disaster risk reduction uses quantitative catastrophe risk profiles. Risk profiles offer crucial information for the creation of practical disaster risk reduction (DRR) policies, as well as for climate change adaptation and national development plans, when combined with data on disaster losses and risk-sensitive budget reviews. The quantitative findings enable cross-country comparison, which contributes to the provision of important data for transboundary risk management.

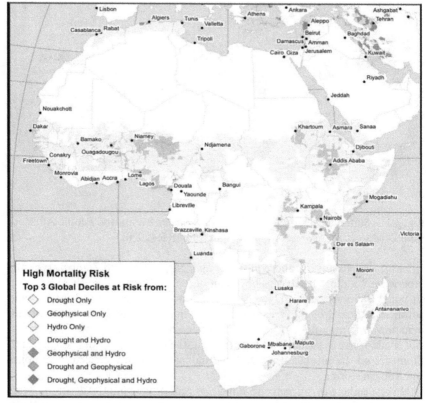

Fig. 3.2.   Disasters and Country Mortality Risk. *Source*: EMDAT (2010).

In nations with mountainous terrain, high rainfall, soil erosion, and deforestation as a result of irresponsible land management, the risk of landslides is significant. Tropical storms and cyclones mostly strike Madagascar, Mozambique,
and the islands in nations around the southeastern coast of the Indian Ocean.
Storms frequently result in significant losses and destruction, especially during
the southwest Indian Ocean cyclone season (November–May). The El Nino
Southern Oscillation phenomenon may be responsible for a number of extreme
hydro-meteorological events across the continent. Extreme events will probably
occur more frequently and with greater intensity as a result of climate change
(Inter-governmental Panel on Climate Change (IPCC), 2007).

Countries from Eritrea to Mozambique that are located along the Rift Valley are particularly susceptible to earthquakes. Many volcanoes, like Mount
Nyiragongo in the Democratic Republic of the Congo and Mount Karthala
in the Comoros, are known to be active along the Rift Valley and on islands
in the Indian Ocean. Many coastal nations, especially those with low-lying
metropolitan centres like the heavily populated Niger delta and low-lying
locations along the coasts of West and East Africa as well as Madagascar,

are growingly concerned about sea-level rise. According to recent studies, tsunami risk is higher in low-lying nations around the Indian Ocean coast (UNISDR, 2009).

3.4. Vulnerability and Systematic Risk

Due to poverty, a heavy reliance on rain-fed agriculture, and constrained institutional capacities, the majority of countries have low coping ability. Natural catastrophes disproportionately affect the poor, as is widely known (UNISDR, 2009). Natural catastrophes frequently have a higher impact on poor countries, which includes economies that are small and susceptible, such as many small island states, countries that are landlocked, and many African nations. It is frequently difficult for them to rebuild after a significant disaster, which further reduces their capacity to build disaster resilience.

Systemic risk is described as 'risk that is endogenous to, or ingrained in, a system that is not itself recognized to be a risk and is therefore not normally tracked or controlled' by the UNDRR. In sub-Saharan Africa, systemic risk puts efforts to end poverty and promote sustainable development in jeopardy. In sub-Saharan Africa, a variety of factors, including transboundary shocks, demographic issues related to urbanisation, climate change, poverty, and violence, influence systemic risk. Cascading patterns of risk are created by the interaction and synthesis of several components. For instance, rural poverty encourages a reliance on natural resources as well as fast urbanisation (which might overwhelm municipal authorities and also degrade rural ecosystems). Conflict and fragility also frequently worsen. Similar to how war and fragility increase underlying vulnerability through displacement and have an influence on health, the delivery of basic services, and people's ability to overcome poverty, they also tend to amplify the effects of natural disasters (UNDRR, 2020).

The value of a systems-based approach to risk governance that considers risk patterns and the multi-sectoral consequences of interactions between human and non-human systems must be made clear. Additionally, there is a need to pay specific attention to underlying vulnerability. Investing in early warning systems, creating risk transfer mechanisms, and establishing social protection programmes at the national and regional levels with the assistance of the Regional Economic Communities are further strategies for tackling systemic risk in the region (UNDRR, 2020).

Poverty and structural problems on the African continent are factors that contribute to and express the region's vulnerability to disasters and are mostly highlighted as follows:

(A) *Limited fiscal resources and weak economic resilience:*

Although many Sub-Saharan African nations' economic performance has improved, their fiscal resources and investment potential in DRR measures are constrained. *Ex ante* public investments in DRR must compete with other needs including debt repayment, infrastructure, defense, and healthcare. Africa is home to 33 countries with a significant debt burden that are either completely or partially eligible for the heavily indebted poor countries (HIPC) initiative (IDA and IMF, 2009).

(B) *Reliance on rain-fed agriculture*:

Numerous Sub-Saharan African nations heavily rely on agriculture that is supported by rainfall for their economy. This industry is especially exposed to the high levels of inter- and intra-annual climate fluctuation and, consequently, to possible climate change. Fig. 3.2 shows how gross domestic product (GDP) development in Ethiopia historically closely tracked changes in rainfall, serving as a representative example for many nations on the continent that heavily rely on rainfall agriculture. Any drought may severely affect people's livelihoods and economies as a whole.

(C) *Inadequacy of infrastructure to respond to and recover from climate change and to mitigate its effects:*

In comparison to other continents, Africa has relatively little infrastructure to protect against hydro-meteorological phenomena. Only about 200 m^3 of water may be stored annually per person in Africa. While North America has an average water storage capacity of 5,961 m^3/person/year, countries like Ethiopia, for instance, have a water storage capacity of about 43 m^3/person/year (World Bank, 2010). Infrastructure, such as safe roads, schools, and hospitals, is necessary to provide the populace with essential services. They turn into essential infrastructure for rescue and recovery efforts in the immediate wake of disasters. In order for them to withstand specific earthquakes, cyclones, or flood occurrences, transportation infrastructure, educational facilities, and healthcare facilities must be built and maintained to minimal standards. Building regulations and standards are frequently not followed, which may result in higher costs for construction.

(D). *Weak governance and institutional capacities*:

Sub-Saharan African nations have a difficult time establishing an institutional and regulatory framework that would allow them to respond to disasters and manage risk mitigation measures. The institutional framework addressing DRM across many ministries and agencies is unclear, there is a lack of adequate staffing and skills, inadequate analytical and implementation ability, and there are weak linkages with other agencies and academia, non-governmental organisations, and the corporate sector. The majority of countries' disaster risk management policies and laws take an *ex post* response to disasters and frequently lack the appropriate techniques, tools, or an *ex ante* approach to risk reduction.

Only a few African nations have a legal and institutional framework in place that incorporates DRR into comprehensive development plans that take into account all hyogo framework for action (HFA) pillars. Even well-equipped national DRM agencies frequently lack essential funds to purchase vehicles, early warning systems, or communications equipment. At sub-national and local levels, where remote district offices rely on financing and information from capitals, funding for DRM authorities is especially scarce.

(E) *Limited knowledge base*:

The capacities of many DRM groups in Africa are constrained, primarily as a result of a lack of skilled officials and less so as a result of a lack of technology. On the continent, graduate programmes for DRM specialists are uncommon, and some colleges, like Bahir Dar University in Ethiopia, have just started offering specific degrees.

In most nations, there is a dearth of expertise in early warning systems, remote sensing, risk insurance, and hydro-meteorological services. Recent efforts to improve hydro-meteorological services across the continent have revealed numerous flaws in the observation networks, telecommunications, and informatics systems as well as inadequate data handling capabilities (IRI, 2006). Even little information is available to evaluate other threats (such as geological tools and professionals who can monitor earthquakes).

3.5. Systematic Risk Reduction Recommendations

- Replace interventions that focus on a specific hazard with measures that take into account all potential vulnerabilities.
- Invest in initiatives that try to deal with the fundamental causes of vulnerability.
- Enhance early warning systems, paying attention to flimsy signals like the accumulation of minor threats, to better connect information to action.

3.6. Population Growth in Hazard-prone Urban Areas

Sub-Saharan Africa is increasingly exposed to natural hazards due to factors like population growth and rapid urbanisation. African nations are rapidly urbanising: from 33 million in 1950 to 548 million in 2018, the urban population in Africa increased 16 times; it is anticipated to increase by 50% (824 million) by 2030 and triple (1,489 million) by 2050. (UNDRR, 2020). Cities with growth rates of more than 4% annually include Nairobi, Niamey, Dar es Salaam, and Lomé (UN-Habitat, 2008). Typically, urban regions are the hubs of economic resources and development engines for the economy. Urban regions' susceptibility to risks is a result of a number of factors, including unsustainable production and consumption patterns, stress on ecosystems, climate change, and other factors. Similar to other emerging nations, growing urbanisation in Africa is resulting in substantial ecological harm, including habitat loss, deforestation, and altered hydrological cycles, which increases the risk of natural disasters. The vulnerability of urban populations to disaster hazards is often exacerbated by poverty and unequal access to essential amenities. For example, lack of affordable housing and transportation options forces many African cities' citizens to live in unofficial settlements near floodplains and unstable hillsides (UNDRR, 2020). Urban areas are frequently found along low-lying river deltas or on coastlines that are vulnerable to flood, coastal surge, and sea-level rise. Numerous African cities are impacted by urban flooding (see also PDNAs in Dakar, Ouagadougou, and Bangui). Large portions of the urban population are exposed to natural disasters because of inadequate infrastructure, poor urban governance, and lack of construction regulations. Particularly in the case of the quickly expanding informal settlements, this is true.

3.7. Climate Change: Possible Impacts in Developing Economies

The term 'climate change' refers to the anticipated significant changes in our climate that may be directly attributable to an increase in greenhouse gas emissions caused by humans. The Fourth Assessment Report of the IPCC (2007) included a number of climate projection scenarios that indicated expected temperature increases, changes in precipitation patterns, sea-level rise, and cyclone activity (Dasgupta et al., 2009). The estimates provided by several general climate models (GCMs) serve as the foundation for these climate projections. According to IPCC (2007), all scenarios and model results forecast a temperature increase in this century between 1.5°C and 4°C. By the end of the twenty-first century, projected sea-level rise would have an influence on low-lying coastal communities, as well as worsen storm surges, salinate coastal areas, and alter delta habitats. Although GCMs show variations in precipitation patterns, there are significant model differences in the trends, magnitudes, and impacted regions. Projections of the associated run-off, river flow, or groundwater recharge are even more challenging. Although there has been very little 'downscaling' of GCMs to a regional or national level, it would be helpful to address the likely impacts for planning purposes. Climate change is predicted to result in more intense hydro-meteorological phenomena. Climate change has already had a substantial impact on the geographic distribution, frequency, and intensity of risks, according to IPCC (2007). The last 20 years have seen 6 of Africa's 10 warmest years on record, and the average temperature increased by roughly 0.5°C throughout that time.

3.8. Economic and Social Impacts of Disasters in Emerging Economies

Disasters frequently have significant negative effects on the economy and society, resulting in short- and long-term economic losses, expensive reconstruction and recovery costs, and furthering the relationship between catastrophe risk and poverty. Including epidemics, there were 8,866 disaster events between 1975 and 2008 that resulted in 2.28 million fatalities and $1,527.7 billion in economic losses worldwide (UNISDR, 2008). The majority of the absolute costs during this time were borne by high-income nations (North America, Europe, and portions of Asia), yet Africa reported the greatest number of victims. However, it becomes evident that the burden on high-income countries is significantly smaller than on middle- and low-income countries when economic repercussions are assessed in relation to the countries' GDP. Small and susceptible economies, such as many small island states and landlocked nations, are more frequently affected by natural disasters than major economies.

The increased frequency of natural disaster occurrences in the Southern African region is a major contemporary issue. Beneficiary needs must be met due to the severity of the damage caused by these disasters in order to lessen the hardships that will follow and the loss of life in the affected communities, as detailed in Table 3.1. Bush fires, floods, sickness and epidemic outbreaks, as well as droughts, have all occurred in Southern Africa as a result of natural disasters. These have caused fatalities and injuries, as well as the displacement of many impacted populations, leaving them vulnerable to starvation and despair (UN, 2009).

Relief organisations are now required to respond quickly, effectively, and efficiently to an increasing variety of natural disaster occurrences, the frequency of disaster occurrences has increased, creating more problems for them. As an illustration, cyclones Connie and Eline, which struck the South Coast of Mozambique in February 2000 and expanded to sections of Malawi, Zambia, and Zimbabwe, left a path of destruction in their wake. Approximately 120,000 homes were displaced by Cyclone Favio in Madagascar and Mozambique in 2007 (Lukamba, 2010), while up to 3.6 million people in Malawi, Zambia, and Lesotho needed food aid as a result of the severe drought situation that occurred in the same years (IFRC World Disasters Report, 2007).

In order to facilitate quick and effective responses, the highest degree of humanitarian supply chain management during relief operations includes tasks like stakeholder management, strategic planning, and assessment initiatives. The initial problem for the aid organisations is finding the required materials from various contributors. The effectiveness of the relief effort is then dependent on implementing the most effective supply chain management techniques in relation to crucial operations like procurement, warehousing, transportation, and distribution, as well as planning and execution. As a result, the donated items must be sent to the impacted areas as soon as possible (Perry, 2007).

The necessary goods must be purchased and transported 'in the right quantity, to the right people at the right location, and at competitive costs' in order for relief efforts to be successful. The advantage of achieving supply chain efficiency during humanitarian operations is to minimise the suffering of the impacted communities and to prevent any additional fatalities (Zhao et al., 2002). As a result, the supply chain must be responsive, adaptable, and agile.

3.9. Overview of Disasters Across the Globe

Natural disaster-related economic losses on a global scale are substantial and rising. From an average of $27 billion in 1970–1980 to around $200 billion in 2010–2019, the global annual average loss has increased by an order of magnitude, making annual totals in the hundreds of billions the norm. The build-up of assets in risky places and their rising value, particularly in quickly developing areas like South East Asia, are the main causes of this increase in disaster losses. The two natural disasters that cause the most damage are earthquakes and tropical storms; 2011 still holds the record for being the most expensive owing to the Thoku earthquake and tsunami, followed by 2017 due to its Atlantic hurricane season. The insurance sector has become accustomed to severe years, when numerous catastrophic events take place in a single year.

Natural disasters are occurring more frequently, mostly due to an increase in climate-related dangers, such as floods and storms. Over 80% of danger events between 1979 and 2019 were weather-related. In contrast to the 1980s, the previous 10 years have seen a roughly three-fold increase in the frequency of global floods and a nearly two-fold increase in storm frequency, encompassing tropical, extratropical, and convective storms.

There is compelling evidence that human-induced climate change is increasing the likelihood and severity of some extreme weather events, particularly those related to heat, and that this trend is supported by the scientific area of extreme event attribution. Three studies have linked climate change to a number of recent natural disasters, such as storms, floods, wildfires, and severe temperatures. It is difficult to distinguish a distinct signal of climate change above the noise of natural variability, and the transition from the identification of recent trends in event incidence to climate change attribution is complicated. Recent occurrences and the foreseeable future will witness an increase in the susceptibility of people and property to natural disasters as a result of macrotrends in economic development, population growth, and urbanisation, which continues to be the main cause of rising risk and economic loss.

Disaster exposure in emerging economies is far higher than in industrialised economies. The Caribbean region has suffered the highest losses globally as a share of GDP, while Asia (particularly rapidly developing economies in South East Asia) has been most negatively impacted in terms of disaster frequency and population disruption due to its geographic features and exposure to various natural hazards. Between 1980 and 2015, the average yearly loss from disasters was 1.5% of GDP in emerging markets compared to 0.3% of GDP in established economies. Hazard exposures will change due to climate change in many different parts of the world, but as sea levels rise, low-lying coastal areas will be most at danger. The majority of the world's megacities are located in these regions, which also host one-third of the global population. These regions also have the largest population densities and are experiencing a significant acceleration of urbanisation compared to non-coastal locations.

Developing nations are disproportionately affected by disasters because they are vulnerable to a wide range of risks, which increases their losses during emergencies. Additionally, while the development of the insurance industry is often stronger in economically developed nations, these economies have less protection against natural disasters. In rich nations, about 40% of direct natural disaster losses are typically insured, compared to less than 10% in middle-income nations and less than 5% in low-income nations.

Investing in resilience-building initiatives can lessen the severity of the impact and the improvement in recovery results. By providing more security and stability, increased resilience can in turn encourage economic innovation and growth. A crucial and economical method to increase resilience is risk transfer through the purchase of insurance. Through timely, efficient, and equitable money distribution in the wake of a catastrophe, insurance lessens the need for *ex post* financial assistance. Nevertheless, due to higher upfront costs, conflicting incentives, a lack of information, and a lack of convincing data to support investment, many nations are hesitant to invest in resilience. Despite this, it is crucial to take into account the compelling and well-established cost-benefit justifications for investing in resilience, which on average outweigh the costs by a factor of four to one.

Table 3.1. Main Disaster Occurrences and the Corresponding Beneficiary Needs.

Disaster Classification	Disaster Occurrence	Main Characteristics	Beneficiary Needs
Hydro-meteorological disasters	Flooding, cyclones, and flash floods	• Massive torrential rains. • Displaces households. • Destroys infrastructure and communication networks. • Limited access and movement between areas	• Relocation to unaffected areas. • Provision of temporary shelter, clothing, and sleeping material. • Provision of food supplies and clean drinking water
	Droughts and widespread starvation	• Acute food shortages triggered by a decline in cereal and crop production. • More communities requiring food aid. • Children are usually the most vulnerable group	• Transportation of food supplies to the affected communities. • Main food supplies on demand – grains, cereals, tinned foods, and high energy biscuits. • Implementation of measures aimed at improving food sustainability
Biological disasters	Epidemic outbreaks	• Outbreaks of diseases such as cholera, typhoid, and malaria. • Need to be properly managed. • Affected individuals need medical and food supplies	• Provision of medical care and supplies to affected areas. • Implementation of measures to prevent the diseases from spreading. • Provision of consistent medical and food supplies

Source: Adapted from Holloway (2003), Lukamba (2010, p. 483), OCHA (2013, p. 5), Mbohwa (2010), and UNICEF (2008).

3.10. Emerging Economies: Recovering from Disasters

Whether the post-disaster 'normal' is a return to the same status as before the catastrophe, or whether recovery has sparked the improvement of an economic or social system to boost resilience, the quality of recovery is a measure of the change in resilience. Along with economic recovery states, social recovery which may be further divided into amenity and safety must be highlighted. Indicators of amenity include population change, cultural change (such as whether houses have been split up), the availability and calibre of social services, and the state of a community and the services provided therein. In contrast, societal safety is determined by the built environment's susceptibility to hazard occurrences and by attempts to increase resilience, which makes the built environment more resilient to failure and improves a population's ability to deal with a disaster.

3.11. Success and Failure in Recovery Outcomes

In choosing between quality and speed of recovery, there is a consideration of how to accomplish both a quick recovery and a reformative recovery that strengthens resilience. A successful outcome is one that partially satisfies both criteria and recovers relatively quickly to a stable state that is an improvement above the resilience levels prior to the event. For instance, the 2008 magnitude 8.0 Sichuan earthquake required enormous recovery efforts due to the high death toll and economic losses, yet assessments of the reaction and reconstruction efforts have generally been favourable. The Chinese government was able to mobilise government agencies, the private sector, and a larger portion of the population with astounding speed and efficiency. The government also took advantage of the opportunities the disaster presented to rebuild the economy better and further develop it through investment, which led to a significantly better economic outcome. For instance, all public-service facilities in the impacted areas were rebuilt with the use of cutting-edge technology and rigorous seismic standards. However, the quick rebuilding effort was deemed to have worsened the region's amenity because it was rather indifferent to the environment and cultural character of the area.

The calculation of recovery quality takes into account both amenity and safety results. Numerous disasters, as was already mentioned, are shown to lead to better safety and physical resilience measures. The government demonstrated significant leadership in putting the initiative to 'build back better' into action in the instance of the Maule catastrophe, which destroyed almost 370,000 homes and had an impact on two million people. Within two years, recovery had made significant progress; 54% of homes had been renovated or rebuilt, and another 30% were under construction. The effective and cooperative nature of post-disaster urban planning which brought together architects/planners, local authorities, academics, and affected individuals and businesses was one of several elements that facilitated a quick recovery.

3.12. Failure to Recover

This is evident in situations that could be viewed as failures because recovery was sluggish and ineffective, leading to social and economic conditions that were worse than they had been before the disaster. A tiny number of severe cases – each of which had severe catastrophic destruction, large losses to stocks of physical buildings and infrastructure, and significant obstacles to recovery were assessed to have never recovered. The 1952 Kamchatka earthquake in Russia and the 1963 Vajont Dam outburst flood in Northern Italy are two examples of cases when society never fully recovered. The affected populations either made the decision to leave the afflicted region on their own or were given instructions to do so. The Vajont Dam, the centrepiece of the Italian government's hydroelectric power project in the foothills of the Alps, was praised in Italy as a demonstration of the country's engineering prowess. A 500 million tonne landslide that collapsed into the lake in October 1963 caused a devastating outburst flood that surged down the valley and killed 1,909 people in a matter of minutes. Reservoir filling had started in 1960, but geological instability had become apparent soon after. After the incident, the authorities relocated survivors into Vajont, a newly constructed village 50 km away, and forbade them from returning. As a result, the devastated area never fully recovered, while the risk for the community that was evacuated was decreased. In addition, the government used the catastrophe to encourage the industrialisation of northeast Italy by providing financial support in the form of company loans and subsidies, raising the region's economic productivity.

In other instances, there was no economic recovery or, at the very least, the economies were severely weak. This includes the 1980 Irpinia earthquake in Italy, which caused 300,000 homeless people and nearly 4,500 fatalities. Major government and international relief donations were made, and the event received much international attention. However, a significant corruption scandal characterised this case. Of the $40 billion allotted for help and recovery, an estimated $20 billion went to a small group of corrupt wealthy people, politicians, and the organised crime organisation.

3.13 References

Balcik, B., Beamon, B. M., Krejci, C. C, Muramatsu, M. K., & Ramirez, B. (2010). Co-ordination in humanitarian relief chains: Practices, challenges and opportunities. *International Journal of Production Economics*, *126*, 22–34.

Dasgupta, S., Laplante, B., Meisner, C. et al. (2009). The impact of sea level rise on developing countries: a comparative analysis. *Climatic Change*, *93*, 379–388. https://doi.org/10.1007/s10584-008-9499-5

EMDAT. (2010). Annual Disaster Statistical Review 2009. In F. Vos, J. Rodriguez, R. Below, D. Guha-Sapir (Eds.), *TheNumbers and Trends*. Brussels: CRED

Holloway, A. (2003). Disaster reduction in Southern Africa. *African Security Review*, *12*(1), 29–38.

Howden, M. (2009, May). *How humanitarian logistics information systems can improve humanitarian supply chains: A view from the field* [Conference proceedings]. Proceedings from the 6th international ISCRAM conference, Gothenburg, Sweden.

IFRC World Disasters Report. (2007). *Focus on information in disasters.* Retrieved September 14, 2013, from http://www.ifrc.org/publicat/wdr2005/

International Monetary Fund (2009). Debt Relief Under the Heavily Indebted Poor Countries (HIPC) Initiative. https://www.imf.org/en/About/Factsheets/Sheets/2023/Debt-relief-under-the-heavily-indebted-poor-countries-initiative-HIPC

IPCC. (2007). AR4 Climate Change 2007: Synthesis Report. https://www.ipcc.ch/report/ar4/syr/

Lukamba, M. T. (2010). Natural disasters in African countries: What can we learn about them? *The Journal of Trans-Disciplinary Research in Southern Africa, 6*(2), 478–495.

Mbohwa, C. (2010). Humanitarian logistics: Review and case study of Zimbabwean experiences. *Journal of Transport and Supply Chain Management, 4,* 176–197.

OCHA. (2013). *Flood season draws to a close.* Retrieved June 12, 2013, from http://rosa.humanitarianresponse.info

Oloruntoba, R., & Gray, R. (2006). Humanitarian aid in agile supply chains. *Supply Chain Management an International Journal, 11*(2), 115–120.

Perry, M. (2007). Natural disaster management planning: A study of logistics managers responding to the Tsunami. *International Journal of Physical Distribution & Logistics Management, 37*(5), 409–433.

The International Research Institute for Climate and Society. (2006). 2004–2006 Report. Columbia University.

UNDRR. (2020). *Highlights: Africa regional assessment report 2020 (forthcoming).* United Nations Office for Disaster Risk Reduction (UNDRR). https://www.undrr.org/publication/highlights-africa-regional-assessment-report-2020

UN-Habitat. (2008). *The State of the African Cities Report 2008.* https://unhabitat.org/the-state-of-the-african-cities-report-2008

UNICEF. (2008). *2004 Disasters and lessons learnt.* Retrieved September 14, 2013, from www.unicef.org/har08/index_tsunami.html

United Nations (UN). (2009). *Strengthening of the coordination of emergency humanitarian assistance of the United Nations* [Report]. Secretary General to the General Assembly Economic and Social Council. Retrieved September 14, 2013, from www.reliefweb.int/rw/RWFILES2009.nsf/FilesByRWDocUnidFilename/SNA-A7U67T3-full_report.pdf/$File/full_report.pdf

United Nations Office for Disaster Risk Reduction. (2008). International day for disaster reduction 2008. https://www.undrr.org/publication/international-day-disaster-reduction-2008

United Nations Office for Disaster Risk Reduction. (2009). Global assessment report on disaster risk reduction 2009. https://www.undrr.org/publication/global-assessment-report-disaster-risk-reduction-2009

World Bank. (2010). The world bank annual report 2010: Year in review. https://openknowledge.worldbank.org/bitstream/handle/10986/5906/WorldBank-AnnualReport2010.pdf?sequence=1

Zhao, X., Xie, J., & Zhang, W. F. (2002). The impact of information sharing and ordering co-ordination on supply chain performance. *Supply Chain Management: An International Journal, 7*(1), 24–40.

Chapter 4

Supply Chain Channels and Network Design

4.1. Introduction

This chapter discusses the strategic planning, distribution channels, and logistics networks in humanitarian logistics in the African context. Disasters can be either natural, resulting from geomorphological or meteorological phenomena, or man-made, including human intention or ignorance and causing misery for people as well as harm to the environment. These create a demand for humanitarian logistics, which are essentially the same as business logistics with the exception of the theatre (Tiwari et al., 2015). Humanitarian logistics refers to the management of the supply chain and logistics in the aid industry. In this industry, there are many parties that are impacted; these parties are referred to as stakeholders.

4.2. Groupings of Stakeholders

Literature from more than 40 peer reviewed sources indicated that the numerous stakeholders involved in the humanitarian supply chain can be grouped as follows:

(1) UN Relief agencies (WFP, UNICEF, etc.).
(2) Government donors (public) (USAID, DFID, etc.).
(3) Corporate donors (private) (Fritz Institute, Aidmatrix, American logistics Aid networks, etc.).
(4) Non-governmental organisations (NGOs) (World Vision, Oxfam, CAR, etc.).
(5) Military such as the US Army and South African defence forces play a pivotal role in getting aid to victims especially with their aircraft and highly terrain adapted vehicles and their skilled personnel.
(6) Manufacturing companies: these can be directed by governments to manufacture certain types of commodities, for example, the American government

Supply Networks in Developing Countries:
Sustainable and Humanitarian Logistics in Growing Consumer Markets, 45–56
Copyright © 2023 by Tatenda Talent Chingono and Charles Mbohwa
Published under exclusive licence by Emerald Publishing Limited
doi:10.1108/978-1-80117-194-620231004

together with the South African government facilitated the cooperation and manufacturing of vaccines to combat the Corona Virus disaster in both countries. American company, Johnson and Johnson authorised the production of their vaccine to South Africa based Aspen to produce and distribute the vaccines to victims.

(7) Victims: these are people directly or indirectly affected by the disaster. They can be considered to be the finale component of humanitarian supply chains. They are the consumers of the aid.

(8) Transporters: especially airline companies, most of the aid comes to Africa via Emirates airlines.

4.3. Supply Network Components of Humanitarian Aid

Transportation, warehousing, inventory control, material handling, order management, customer service packaging, and reverse logistics are all included in humanitarian logistics (United Nations, 2007).

The sponsors and suppliers who provide financial sponsorship, gifts, grants, or supplies like food and non-food items make up the inbound or upstream logistical side. These migrate further down the supply chain as knowledge travels in both directions, from and to the disaster victims. The victims, also known as clients, are divided into relief and development initiatives, communities, or beneficiaries. When responding to natural disasters, there are typically little or no production-related logistics activities, but when it comes to man-made disasters, such the Corona Virus and AIDS, the production of pharmaceutical medications, vaccines, and personal protective equipment is essential to save lives. Supply networks would need to connect the items on the following list: donors, aid organisations, governments, manufacturers, the military, logistics service providers, non-governmental groups, and victims or beneficiaries. Food distribution, water and sanitation, medical assistance, relocations, quarantines, and the supply of temporary housing are examples of common areas of collaboration.

4.4. Characteristics of Humanitarian Logistics

- Ambiguous goals, with humanitarian efforts frequently being spontaneous, unsolicited, and desperate on the part of donors, agencies, the media, and beneficiaries.
- High uncertainty that depends on assessment of ongoing changes in supply and demand.
- Humanitarian interventions after a disaster are typically marked by acute urgency.
- A highly politicised environment, from donations through distribution in the field.
- Limited resources with high employee turnover in staff, heavy physical and emotional demands, limited funding with challenges relating to cash flow, and frequently severely damaged infrastructure (Mellat-Parast & Spillan, 2014; Mentzer et al., 2001; Van Wassenhove, 2006).

4.5. Humanitarian Logistics Versus Commercial Logistics

According to Mentzer et al. (2001), there is a difference between commercial supply chains and humanitarian logistics in that the former place more emphasis on yield, ensuring that recipients receive the greatest possible benefit. Commercial supply chain management focusses on customer satisfaction versus beneficial survival or saving lives which is central to humanitarian logistics. The World Bank (2001) also goes further and highlights the deliberate volunteering in humanitarian operations as opposed to corporate social responsibility in the business world and motivators for humanitarian action. According to Oxfam (2007), importance of the mission is key to serving lives as opposed to achievement of profit in commercial logistics.

4.6. Humanitarian Operations

Humanitarian logistics are divided into three categories: preparation, urgent reaction, and reconstruction. Preparation includes risk management and disaster prevention. They focus on crisis management which is the immediate response; reconstruction is continuity and preparation.

Humanitarian operations deal with more than just disasters; they also address emergency relief or response to disasters, such as providing temporary shelters, distributing food, distributing gifts-in-kind like clothing, medical supplies, and school supplies, as well as development and support activities like constructing schools and clinics.

4.7. Disaster Management

According to Mandal (2016), the goal of humanitarian operations is to prevent catastrophes from happening in the first place and to ensure that the right procedures are in place to lessen the effects of possible disasters, which will prevent injuries and fatalities from occurring before they happen. The cycle of steps outlined below is crucial for the accomplishment of humanitarian missions:

Preparedness: entails developing capacities, working with communities, and conducting drills for evacuation. Appropriate professionals should be hired; they should also be prepared to be deployed quickly. Prepare supplies for relief in various sites throughout the world. To stop expensive and unregulated purchasing, framework agreements must be codified.

Response: activated as soon as a crisis occurs. To save lives, the first 72 hours are crucial. Different organisations respond in different ways. For example, World Vision provides children with shelter, safety, and care. The Red Cross saves lives as quickly as possible. It is the most crucial stage. Ensures that the appropriate food, housing, and medical supplies are offered. Transport is essential but can be expensive. It may be severely jeopardised, particularly if the road infrastructure has been harmed (Oloruntoba & Gray, 2006).

Transition phase: enables more targeted support and more accurate supply and demand forecasts. The replenishment of supplies at prepositioned facilities occurs as the transition from quick response to extended recovery and mitigation occurs (Murray, 2005).

Recovery: communities receive assistance in re-enacting earlier circumstances. Takes from months to years. Training, capacity building, infrastructure improvement, home reconstruction, and service delivery at the previous level are all included.

Mitigation: boosting community awareness and preparedness to lessen the effects of calamities. Implement technical early-warning support systems and plant plants to help mitigate flood damage. Little logistical assistance is required (Van Wassenhove, 2006).

The preparedness and reaction phases are when humanitarian logistics is most apparent.

4.8. Humanitarian Supply Chains

Recently, supply chain configuration has drawn more and more interest from researchers and practitioners alike. In 2015, Nepal was devastated by a destructive 7.8M earthquake; many homes and lives were destroyed. Governments and allies had to band together in order to salvage the remnants and support those who most needed it. This book proposes an integrated model for creating and improving international and national logistics networks in order to save lives as a result of several similar incidents, whether man-made disaster, which is caused by human intent, negligence, error, or accident. It has a data mapping section and a mixed integer linear programming model. It has been specifically designed to address the configuration challenge for supply chains that are unique in their level of complexity and unpredictability relative to actual global logistics networks (Russel, 2005).

Even while this topic is widely understood and well-explained technically in the literature that is currently available, it still presents challenges in reality, particularly when it comes to coping with real-life complexity, service level restrictions, and data mapping. We created our integrated approach in order to close these gaps. We specifically created our model to handle multiple-layer, single-location layer, multiple-commodity, and time-constrained logistics networks, and we designed it to be deployed in a deterministic environment with a single period time horizon. The suggested method facilitates the data collection and processing tasks, which are generally acknowledged as being difficult and time-consuming tasks for the management of logistical activities. It also constitutes a new contribution to the body of existing scientific knowledge.

4.9. Generic Humanitarian Supply Chains

For a variety of services, including development projects, food distribution, in-kind gift distribution, and emergency relief or response, there are numerous supply chains. Fig. 4.1 shows how supply chains are built from the ground up.

Since supply chain strategy deals with choices that have a long-term impact on a company, it is a crucial place to start for sustainable healthcare supply chain (HSC) management. There is a lot of research on supply chain management. Frameworks for picking the best supply chain strategies can be based on the types

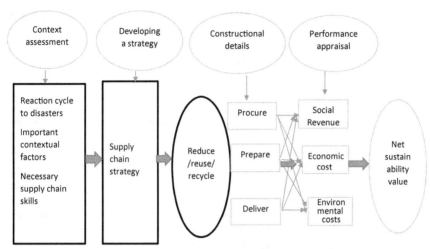

Fig. 4.1.   Supply Chain Formulation Framework. *Source*: Adapted from Chen et al. (2020).

of products (e.g., 'efficient' for 'functional' vs 'responsive' for 'innovative') or into a 2×2 matrix for matching supply chain strategies (e.g., 'efficient', 'responsive', 'risk-hedging', and 'agile') with supply and demand uncertainty. In several scenarios, Chen et al. (2020) suggested integrating lean and agile hybrid supply chain techniques. Researchers propose identifying and reducing low-probability, high-impact risks to manage unanticipated supply chain disruptions. These studies, despite the insightful information they provided, all concentrated on commercial supply chains. The supply chain techniques they suggested are not immediately applicable to the humanitarian context because health organisations (HOs) do not produce goods or pursue profits, and they engage in rivalry in other ways. Furthermore, since the setting is considerably different from commercial operations, building entirely new supply chains for humanitarian responses immediately following a disaster involves more than just a novel application of existing theories. The unique aspects of the humanitarian environment must be taken into consideration when designing sustainable HSC initiatives (Chen et al., 2020).

Usually, there are four generic supply chains:

(1) *Continuous replenishment supply chain*: management is made simple by close customer cooperation and relatively predictable demand from established clients.
(2) *Lean supply chain*: consistent demand that is fairly predictable and forecastable, put efficiency first. (Food distribution, possibly predictable given prior demand).
(3) *An agile supply chain is typically unplanned.* They may arise as a consequence of marketing campaigns, new product launches, promotions, or unanticipated possibilities. It considers the inclusion and calculation of services costs. (For

example, adapting to unanticipated/unplanned demand). It is mostly used in disaster and emergency situations to get aid quickly to victims.

(4) *Fully flexible supply chain:* unplanned and unpredictable demand due to unknown customers with exceptional/emergency demands.

Humanitarian supply chains need to be adaptable and quick. Although it shifts from a crucial reaction phase to an ongoing reconstruction phase, the initial scenario in catastrophe circumstances typically dictates the demand for a fully flexible supply chain.

The objective is to provide survivors with access to life-saving supplies as they frequently don't have a choice in their purchasing decisions. Whatever is presented to them must be accepted. As the competencies needed for sustainable operations are context-specific, the accompanying Fig. 4.2 can be helpful in deciding which of the above methods can be adopted depending on unpredictability and urgency.

According to Chen et al. (2020), the required supply speed is determined by the urgency in the operating context. The ability to respond fast is necessary in highly critical situations, such as an earthquake or the sudden start of civil war, in order to activate and deploy resources to provide emergency help. Focus can be switched to cost-efficiency in low urgency settings, such as the recovery and rebuild stage of a catastrophe response. Efficiency and responsiveness have a trade-off relationship. The pursuit of efficiency typically results in rising rigidity and decreasing responsiveness. Cost efficiency is frequently attained through standardisation and size of operations, both of which tend to make the processes more established and difficult to modify. Supply sufficiency is impacted by operational context uncertainty. The degree of predictability is evaluated in relation to the typical time frame for planning and preparing for disaster responses. In low-unpredictability settings (such as long-term health care programmes), HOs have ample time to plan their budgets and acquire the necessary materials in order to get ready for the humanitarian

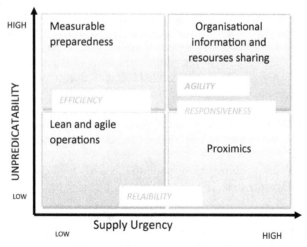

Fig. 4.2.   Context-contingent Sustainable Supply Chain Capabilities.

missions. Efficiency and dependability qualities are desired in these circumstances. The ability to be flexible is necessary to obtain the required supply without a lengthy planning and preparation time horizon in unpredictable scenarios (such as transitioning from emergency relief to sustaining relief and recovery stages). Flexibility and dependability are complementary skills. In order for the service level to be trustworthy and not compromised throughout the dynamic transitions when the supply chain is modified to serve unforeseen missions, reliability is the necessary basis upon which flexibility must be constructed.

4.10. The Generic Supply Chain

The overarching supply chain strategies and the procure, prepare, deliver, and reduce/reuse/recycle (R3) processes are the structural elements. Physical assets, IT systems, organisational missions, and policies are all part of the infrastructure. Supply types upstream include in-kind donations, ad hoc procurement, and prepositioned safety stock. In the downstream, the supply chain may benefit the beneficiaries directly or indirectly through intermediaries like implementing partners. The section focusses on procure, prepare, and deliver's structural elements (Chen et al., 2020). The main configurability elements of the humanitarian supply chain are depicted in Fig. 4.3.

HSCs typically do not involve product design, manufacturing, product take-back, or remanufacturing, according to the justification. The total quality management approach's preference for preventive over corrective measures is also consistent with incorporating the R3 principles into the structural configurations

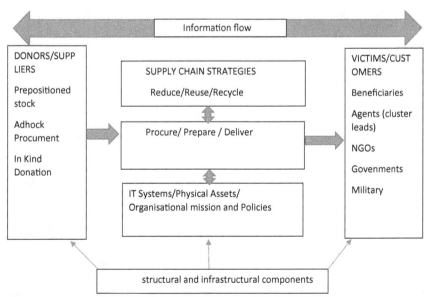

Fig. 4.3.   The Key Configurative Components of the Humanitarian Supply Chain.

of process design. Following are some examples of how the R3 principles are applied in HSCs and how they will be used in the design whenever appropriate. (1) *Reduce*: reduce material consumption/packaging by sharing and pooling, reduce energy consumption and pollution by shortening travel distance and using less energy-intensive transport modes, and reduce non-value adding processes and activities; (2) *Reuse*: buy used instead of new, rent instead of buy, increase material versatility for multiple uses; and (3) *Recycle*: repurpose excess supply, recover residual value, and dispose of waste responsibly.

4.11. Performance Measurement

While commercial/business supply chains aim to maximise profit and return on investment, humanitarian supply chains put a greater emphasis on yield to ensure that beneficiaries receive the greatest possible benefit. When measuring HL, this is one important indicator to take into account. Determining if the appropriate item was supplied at the appropriate time, location, and cost is a key step; making ensuring and measuring important programme results are essential. In the relief industry, performance metrics and measurement systems have not yet been created and widely used. In fact, humanitarian supply chains can use performance measurement frameworks from commercial or business logistics.

The fundamental questions in both commercial and humanitarian logistics are:

What metrics (standards of measurement by which the effectiveness, performance, or progress of a plan, process, or product may be evaluated) are the most effective to use? What connections exist between the information flow decision variables and the performance metrics? How different measurements are included into a single measurement system. These inquiries result in performance matrices for resources, outputs, and flexibility. It is crucial to guarantee that gifts are used for the intended goal of saving lives and easing human suffering in order to secure donor support, which primarily depends on some form of accountability.

4.12. Supply Chain Management Practices Applicable During Humanitarian Relief Operations

Given the difficulties mentioned above that arise during humanitarian catastrophe operations, it is essential to identify and establish a framework of supply chain procedures that will guarantee that disaster operations are carried out effectively and efficiently. Due to their emphasis on the needs of the consumer, concepts addressing agility, flexibility, and responsiveness have been found to be pertinent. These ideas are important, according to researchers, since they help organisations better respond to shifting client needs. Utilising the supply chain idea of postponement, having access to virtual integration capabilities, and successfully coordinating all activities are essential for achieving agility.

Agility refers to the capacity of an organisation to function successfully in a volatile and ever-changing market environment. This indicates that any arising uncertainty can be absorbed and contained by the organisation's supply chain. According to Vonderembse et al. (2006), context-specific agile supply chains allow organisations to quickly react to a changing, dynamic, and highly uncertain environment. This is especially important for disaster relief efforts.

Postponement: Activities are only carried out under the notion of postponement in supply chain management after particular customer orders are received. It is a principle closely related to agility that is typically applied by businesses that deal with uncertainty and is seen as a necessary step in achieving client responsiveness. The majority of the time, postponement is used as an agility tool in inventory management procedures, whereby humanitarian organisations store inventories of particular generic products that are later customised in response to the needs of the impacted people.

Virtual integration: The ability of the organisation to apply improved process control procedures and to manage demand volatility is ensured by virtual integration. It is a typical technique that emphasises inter-organisational coordination, information processing, and management in supply chains to reduce environmental unpredictability and achieve agility. The deployment of IT systems to support shared activities between response stakeholders, such as purchasing, logistics, and distribution, is required for supply chains to be regarded as agile and responsive. By creating a unified information environment with broad and precise communication services, virtual structures provide greater speed and flexibility (Camarinha-Matos & Afsarmanesh, 2004).

Coordination: According to Moeiny and Mokhlesi (2011), 'coordination' refers to a situation in which all organisations providing humanitarian aid and their stakeholders are willing to exchange information that is crucial during relief operations. On the basis of data provided by vendors, the donor community, and their partners, coordination mechanisms make sure that all organisations and parties involved in crisis management make informed decisions. While the majority of freely exchanged information focusses on beneficiary preferences and demand levels, when many partners are involved in analysing the needs of the beneficiaries, there is typically an accurate reflection of the precise needs (Oloruntoba, 2007).

Supply chain flexibility: defined in terms of mobility, uniformity, and range, referring to the various states in which a system can adopt and be capable of switching efficiently from producing one product to another (Jangga et al., 2015). It is said to affect specific organisational components such as the product mix and volume. This suggests that the company can supply and assemble a variety of goods within a predetermined range (Stevenson & Spring, 2007, p. 687). Although manufacturing organisations are where the idea of flexibility originated, efforts have been made to use this idea in service and humanitarian organisations (Krajewski et al., 2005).

Agility and flexibility: Improved responsiveness of the organisation in meeting client needs is the goal of agility and flexibility. In a setting, where consumer needs are subject to quick change, the structure of agile, responsive, and adaptable supply chains is appropriate for implementation (Chandra & Grabis, 2009). Due to the unpredictable timing, type, and scale of catastrophe occurrences, a number of issues pose the biggest problems during disaster operations (Bean et al., 2011). Despite these obstacles, the primary goal of humanitarian organisations is to react quickly to any disasters that occur, which can be accomplished by putting out fast, adaptable, and responsive efforts (Christopher & Towill, 2001). New challenges came with globalisation (supply chains crossing borders) and these include:

(1) *Global sourcing trends*: opportunities for cost savings, revenue growth, and greater dependability.
(2) *Quality trends*: as completion originations rise, attention should be paid to better pre-, transactional, and post-transactional services.
(3) Trends in decision-making for greater profitability, improved supplier lead-time performance, fast delivery, cost reduction, and waste elimination.
(4) *Supply chain agility trends* stay flexible and overcome unforeseen obstacles. These are primarily impacted by manufacturing flexibility, distribution or logistics flexibility, and incumbent or sourcing flexibility.
(5) Ensuring strong cooperation and coordination among all business operations along the extended supply chain by connecting and automating them.
(6) Advanced technology for better manufacturing and forecasting.

4.13. Conclusions and Future Research

Since they emphasise putting the needs of the customer first, supply chain management concepts like agility, adaptability, and responsiveness are relevant (Aprile et al., 2005; Stevenson & Spring, 2007). According to the theory, if identical procedures were used in the supply chains for humanitarian aid used in relief efforts, this would lead to a quicker, more effective response. The procedures of the humanitarian supply chains in Southern Africa, which lag behind those in the commercial sphere, have not received much attention from research. However, the difference between the two has been noted as a determinant in how well their supply chains function and may have a negative influence on the suffering of the impacted populations and the loss of life.

A natural starting point for the multidisciplinary discussion of sustainability is supply chain management. It does so in three ways: (1) first, it offers a holistic structure to integrate various research streams into one cohesive system rooted in practice-based operations; (2) it facilitates multi-level analysis and synthesis both horizontally along the supply chain and vertically across organisational hierarchies; and (3) it provides a standardised common language for cross-sectoral communication because nearly all types of organisational activities managing flows of goods and services can be described in this way (Chen et al., 2020). Supply chain management is a perfect starting place for interdisciplinary enrichment, transdisciplinary learning, and multidisciplinary communication in sustainability research because of these features.

4.14. References

Aprile, D., Garavelli, A. C., & Giannoccaro, I. (2005). Operations planning and flexibility in a supply chain. *Journal of Production Planning and Control, 16*(1), 21–31.

Bean, W. L., Viljoen, N. M., Ittmann, W. H., & Kekana, E. (2011). Disaster management and humanitarian logistics: A South African perspective. *Journal of Transportation and Supply Chain Management, 5*, 39–51.

Camarinha-Matos, L. M., Afsarmanesh, H. (2004). The Emerging Discipline of Collaborative Networks. In L. M. Camarinha-Matos (Eds.), *Virtual Enterprises and Collaborative Networks. PRO-VE 2004. IFIP International Federation for Information Processing* (vol 149). Boston, MA: Springer. https://doi.org/10.1007/1-4020-8139-1_1

Chandra, C., & Grabis, J. (2009). Configurable supply chain: Framework, methodology and application. *International Journal of Manufacturing Technology and Management, 17*(1/2), 5–22.

Chen, H. S. Y., Van Wassenhove, L. N., & Cheng, T. C. E. (2020). Designing sustainable humanitarian supply chains. OSF Preprints m82ar, Center for Open Science. DOI: 10.31219/osf.io/m82ar

Christopher, M., & Towill, D. (2001). An integrated model for the design of agile supply chain. *International Journal of Physical Distribution & Logistics Management, 31*(4), 235–246. https://doi.org/10.1108/09600030110394914

Jangga, R., Ali, N. M., Ismail, M., & Shari, N. (2015). Effect of environmental uncertainty and supply chain flexibility towards supply chain innovation: An exploratory study. *Procedia Economics and Finance, 31,* 262–268.

Krajewski, L., Wei, J. C., & Tang, L. (2005). Responding to schedule changes in build-to order supply chains. *Journal of Operations Management, 23,* 452–469.

Mandal, S. (2016). Towards an integrated logistics capabilities model of supply chain flexibility: A social exchange perspective. *Romanian Economic and Business Review, 11*(3), 44–67.

Mellat-Parast, M., & Spillan, J. E. (2014). Logistics and supply chain process integration as a source of competitive advantage. *The International Journal of Logistics Management, 25,* 289–314.

Mentzer, J. T., Keebler, J. S., Nix, N. W., Smith, C. D., & Zacharia, Z. G. (2001). Defining supply chain management. *Journal of Business Logistics, 22*(2), 1–25.

Moeiny, E., & Mokhlesi, J. (2011). *Management of Relief Supply Chain & Humanitarian Aids through Supply Chain Resilience.* Master Thesis. University College of Boras, School of Engineering.

Murray, S. (2005, January 7). How to deliver on the promises: Supply chain logistics—Humanitarian agencies are learning lessons from business in bringing essential supplies to regions hit by the tsunami. *Financial Times,* 9.

Oloruntoba, R. (2007). Bringing Order Out Of Disorder: Exploring Complexity in Relief Supply Chains. In U. Laptane (Ed.), *Proceedings of the 2nd International Conference on Operations and Supply Chain Management: Regional and Global Logistics and Supply Chain Management* (pp. 1–16). New UM Ad Co Ltd, CD Rom.

Oloruntoba, R., & Gray, R. (2006). Humanitarian aid: An agile supply chain? *Supply Chain Management, 11*(2), 115–120.

Oxfam. (2007). *Climate alarm: Disasters increase as climate change bites* [Briefing Paper, No. 108]. Oxfam.

Russel, T. (2005). *The humanitarian relief supply chain: Analysis of the 2004 South East Asia earthquake and tsunami* [MA thesis]. MIT Center for Transportation and Logistics, Cambridge, MA. http://ctl.mit.edu/metadot/index.pl?id=6156

Samii, R., & Van Wassenhove, L. (2003). The United Nations Joint Logistics Centre (UNJLC): The genesis of a humanitarian relief coordination platform [Case Study 02/2003-5093]. INSEAD, Fontainebleau. https://www.thecasecentre.org/products/view?id=8159

Stevenson, M., & Spring, M. (2007). Flexibility from a supply chain view perspective: Definition and review. *International Journal of Operations and Production Management, 27*(7), 685–713.

Tiwari, A. K., Tiwari, A., & Samuel, C. (2015). Supply chain flexibility: A comprehensive review. *International Journal of Retail & Distribution Management, 38*(7), 767–792.

United Nations. (2007). *Disaster risk reduction: 2007 global review.* UN International Strategy for Disaster Reduction.

Van Wassenhove, L. (2006). Humanitarian aid logistics: Supply chain management in high gear. *Journal of the Operational Research Society, 57*(5), 475–489.

Vonderembse, M. A., Uppal, M., Huang, S. H., Dismukes, J. P. (2006). Designing supply chains: Towards theory development. *International Journal of Production Economics, 100*(2), 223 -238. https://doi.org/10.1016/j.ijpe.2004.11.014.

World Bank. (2001). Attacking poverty, Development report 2000/2001. World Bank.

Chapter 5

Supply Chain Systems and Disaster Management

5.1. Introduction

The chapter defines, explains the various concepts used in disaster management. The concepts explained include: disaster, hazard, vulnerability, capacity, risk, and disaster management cycle. In addition to the terminologies, the study also seeks to explain the importance of the relief chain including sourcing, inventory, transportation, and warehousing in the humanitarian logistics context. Readers should be able to identify and demonstrate the importance of the relief chain.

5.2. Disasters and Supply Chain Systems

Newspapers, radio stations, and television networks almost always report on disasters that are happening throughout the world. But what exactly is a disaster? The French phrase 'Desastre', which combines the terms 'des', which means bad, and 'aster', which means star, is where the word disaster first appeared. As a result, the phrase means 'bad or evil star'. Disasters are 'a major disruption of a community or society's functioning resulting in extensive human, material, economic, and environmental losses which exceed the capacity of the afflicted community/society to cope using its own resources', according to the United Nations (UN). A disaster is the outcome of the interaction of risk, vulnerability, and a lack of resources or protective measures to lessen the likelihood of danger. A disaster occurs when a risk affects a population that is already at risk and results in harm, deaths, and disruption (Khan et al., 2008). Fig. 5.1 illustrates what a disaster is. It shows that disasters mostly occurs only when hazards and vulnerability meet.

5.3. Disaster Management Cycle

All potential activities, programmes, and actions that might be undertaken before, during, and after a disaster with the intention of preventing a disaster, lessening

Supply Networks in Developing Countries:
Sustainable and Humanitarian Logistics in Growing Consumer Markets, 57–68
Copyright © 2023 by Tatenda Talent Chingono and Charles Mbohwa
Published under exclusive licence by Emerald Publishing Limited
doi:10.1108/978-1-80117-194-620231005

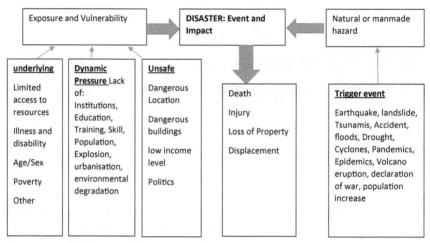

Fig. 5.1.   Explanation of a Disaster.

its impact, or recovering from its losses are collectively referred to as disaster risk management. Fig. 5.2 depicts the emergency response, post-disaster/recovery, and pre-disaster phases of disaster management, along with each phase's constituent parts (disaster mitigation, preparedness, and prevention).

According to Khan et al. (2008), there are three major phases of disaster management and they do not always, or even typically, take place one after the other or in any specific order. The length of each phase mainly depends on the severity of the disaster, and phases of the cycle frequently overlap. As a result, the disaster management circle can be enlarged into seven related stages. For the sake of clarity, some of the components are described below, and Fig. 5.2 shows the management circle:

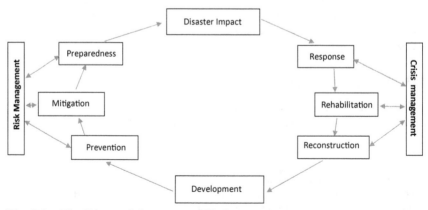

Fig. 5.2.   The Disaster Management Circle.

- *Mitigation*: Reducing the consequences of a tragedy. Examples include zoning laws and building codes, vulnerability assessments, and public education.
- *Preparedness*: Being prepared means figuring out how to react. Examples include emergency plans, drills, and warning systems.
- *Response:* Attempts to reduce the dangers a disaster creates. Examples include search and rescue and disaster aid.
- *Recovery:* Getting the neighbourhood back to normal. Examples include grants, short-term housing, and health treatment.

5.4. Relief Operations and Disaster Management

In general, the disaster management policy responses are influenced by methods and tools for cost-effective and sustainable interventions. Fig. 5.3 depicts how the relief chain can be used to support the disaster management circle.

5.5. Planning and Preparedness

According to the Fritz Institute (2005), this step includes various pre-disaster logistical steps and actions that need to be completed. A plan outlines the activities that need to be completed, who will be responsible for them within the business, and how to obtain the resources that are required. They also need a national or regional plan that takes into account the infrastructure's weaknesses, local logistical resources, and government emergency response capabilities.

Written catastrophe response plans and procedures are part of planning. Governments typically have their own national and local plans that include organisations, duties, priorities, and the primary steps to take in the event of disasters. Numerous scenarios dependent on the severity of the damage are included in the majority of plans. Additionally, humanitarian organisations have their own

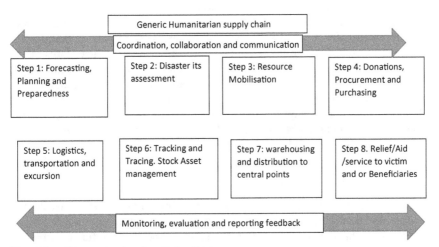

Fig. 5.3.   Humanitarian Logistics Steps.

plans, which are typically coordinated with those of the government but may alternatively be carried out independently (Moeing & Mokhlesi, 2011).

Preparedness: Making the response system ready to handle catastrophic events is connected to preparedness. It is impossible to be totally ready to deal with an earthquake's effects. However, preparation and planning provide a much more efficient response.

Planning for disaster: Organisational, governmental, and international levels all require catastrophe planning. A system of pre-positioning supplies, trucks, and equipment at various hubs throughout the world is run by organisations like the International Federation of Red Cross and Red Crescent Societies, World Vision International, Concern, Oxfam, and numerous UN agencies. These inventories are administered either separately or by the UN Humanitarian Resources Depot.

Assessment of disasters: Disaster assessments serve the functions of demand planning in the chain of aid. After a disaster, evaluation identifies the population's requirements, the infrastructure's capabilities, the extent of the damage, and the local resources that can be mobilised to help. They perform the part of demand estimate and deal with providing the appropriate amount of aid to the appropriate people. They can be carried out using visual inspection, human inquiry, simulation, or sampling. Standard data are used to estimate the effects of catastrophes, such as the potential number of fatalities and injuries, the availability of local resources, and public services like electricity, communications, and transportation. It is challenging to determine what is required, how much is required, when it is required, and where it is required without first conducting a basic assessment (Moeing & Mokhlesi, 2011).

Preparation planning, survey and data collecting, interpretation, forecasting, reporting, and monitoring are a few of the processes that make up assessments in general. The information that has to be acquired is identified during preparation. There are numerous ways to gather data. They include visual inspection, expert interviews, statistical sampling, and checklists.

The necessary parties are informed by an evaluation team of the data analysis and its forecasts for future developments. Since assessments only represent a single point in time, they should be compared to earlier findings. The status of the housing, water, sanitisation, and food systems should be described in the report. It is important to describe the capability and capacity of the local resources that are accessible, as well as any ongoing coordination initiatives. The logistics part should include information on how to provide relief to people, the state of the roads, airports, and seaports, as well as the cost and availability of transportation (Mokhlesi & Moeing, 2011).

5.6. Recourse Mobilisation

An organisation gathers resources and gets things moving before a calamity strikes. As soon as the response operation is in motion, organisations distribute their available resources and start making appealing for further funding. Disaster appeals may be made by a single organisation working on its own or through intermediary organisations like Global Impact. The media is essential in spreading awareness of appeals, which raises awareness of the groups working locally and the needs they have (Moeing & Mokhlesi, 2011).

It is necessary to deploy human resources, which can take the shape of paid aid workers, volunteers, firefighters, ambulance drivers, police officers, or military personnel. Different resources have varying degrees of training, expertise, and connections. Within each organisation as well as between organisations, training differs. Governmental institutions are accustomed to employing people full-time. Non-governmental organisations (NGOs) employ both full-time employees and temporary workers to meet growing demand.

Evidence from 16 African nations demonstrates that 4% of national projected budgets are, on average, allocated for DRR. Only 1% of the national budget, however, is specifically allocated to disaster risk reduction (DRR) interventions. Increasing domestic funding for pre-disaster efforts and DRR investments is crucial for minimising the effects of catastrophes and achieving the Sendai Framework goals. In addition, higher DRR spending would enable governments to rely less on official development assistance (ODA) to meet the needs of their populations after disasters.

Despite continued economic losses resulting from disasters, domestic resources devoted to DRR activities are underfinanced in Africa. Evidence from 16 African countries shows that, on average, 4% of national planned budgets is related to DRR. However, only 1% of the national budget is directly dedicated to DRR interventions. Increasing domestic resources devoted to pre-disaster DRR investments is essential to reduce the impacts of disasters and to achieve the Sendai Framework targets. Furthermore, increased DRR investment would allow governments to reduce reliance on official development assistance to cover the post-disaster needs of their population. Three case studies from Angola, the United Republic of Tanzania, and Zambia are used in this report's evidence to evaluate the costs and advantages of various investment options. Finding and utilising suitable financing options for DRRs is essential. Securing and easing access to funds for catastrophe prevention, reduction, relief, recovery, and reconstruction fall primarily under the purview of governments. For financing (pre- and post-disaster) DRR investment in Africa, a number of mechanisms have been found that use various institutional frameworks for eligibility, access, usage, and governance of the funds they offer.

5.7. Recommendations for Investment in Disaster Relief

- To track advancements and successes, specifically record disaggregated DRR investments in national budgets.
- Create policies to enhance cross-sector investment cooperation.
- Direct financial resources towards initiatives that support national DRR goals and the cool chain association (CCA), sustainable development goals (SDGs), and global DRR frameworks.
- Create structures for incentives to encourage private DRR investment.
- Use a variety of available finance tools to mobilise both domestic and foreign resources.

5.8. Sourcing, Purchasing, and Positioning

Less money spent on decisions including sourcing, buying, and inventory preposi-tioning. Pre-positioning such non-consumable things frequently proves beneficial, and systematically pre-established supply contracts and negotiations with suppli-ers could assure the availability of goods. These organisations should concentrate more on building local sources of supply and agreeing on requirements (Arminas, 2005; Chaikin, 2003). Even though some well-known disaster relief organisations have made great headway on these challenges, other organisations view them as distant objectives or subjects for future thought, which causes the status quo to persist and stagnate. There are still few realistic strategic plans, and there are still operational inefficiencies in the field (Byman et al., 2000). Therefore, creating spe-cialised, in-depth research and strategic evaluations of supply chain management (SCM) components is a potential obstacle to future disaster aid that is effective.

The main focus of inventory management is the control of all completed goods and raw materials in a supply chain. The kind of inventory a company keeps will depend on the type of business it is engaged in. Since inventory invest-ments can reach up to 50% of an organisation's overall investment, it is gener-ally acknowledged that inventory is one of its most expensive assets. Limiting or reducing stock holdings is one method of lowering operating costs. Organisa-tions now have to manage their supply chains more effectively due to high inven-tory expenses.

All organisations are required to maintain some inventory. A manufacturing company may often keep the following categories of inventory on hand: raw mate-rials, finished goods, work-in-progress, machine replacement parts, and inventory travelling (pipeline inventory). As illustrated in Table 5.1, maintaining the right amount of inventory can help with product availability and boost economies of scale during uncertain and volatile times.

5.9. Holding Inventory

The majority of international NGOs keep inventory in order to isolate the pro-duction process from it and maintain a buffer in case of erratic raw material sup-plies when disaster strikes in order to save lives, reduce demand unpredictability, increase customer variety, utilise supplier discounts for large orders, and prevent

Table 5.1.   Importance of Inventory in Different Times and Situations.

Uncertainty	Maintaining inventory is necessary to provide buffers against demand fluctuation and uncertainty
Product availability	During periods of high demand, inventory levels may affect the availability of some products
Economies of scale	Buying inventory in large quantities can save shipping costs and enable cost-cutting while boosting economies of scale

price hikes while the items are in transit, streamline manufacturing demands, and avoid stock-outs.

5.10. Inventory Management Approaches for Humanitarian Logisticians

Sequencing supplies in line (SILS): By using this technique, the line worker is relieved of the responsibility of selecting the appropriate parts for each model of a product, such as a car model. Instead, once each specific model comes online, all required parts are given to match it. For instance, SILS enabled the automaker Vauxhall to flexibly construct two Vauxhall models on the same line in response to market demand.

Kanbans: These are cards or other tools that a station uses to request goods or work from stations earlier in the chain.

Milk runs: This technique makes use of a milk run, which is a route that entails the delivery of shipments and the collection of incoming supplies in the same run or the supplier's daily replenishment of materials. Method of delivery for mixed loads from many providers.

Suplier subassembly by the supplier on the company's property. With this technique, suppliers subassemble parts on the company's property while supplying it. The majority of examples include the provision of pharmaceutical ingredients for treatments like ARVs or the coronavirus vaccine, which must then be further processed into vaccinations and tablets, respectively.

5.11. Gathering Donations

Emergency supplies travel through a variety of routes, formats, and locations to the chain of relief. Giving can take the form of grants, donations, and gifts-in-kind (non-cash goods and/or services). Donations in kind can come in a wide variety of shapes and sizes and come from a wide range of sources. They might or might not have been intended. Planned donations frequently take care of the needs that were identified during the evaluation phase. Unexpected donations might not always be appropriate for the needs of the tragedy.

Goods that are not a priority or that have not been requested are frequently given anonymously. Aid can be bilateral, provided directly from a donor government to a recipient country, or multilateral, managed by international organisations that gather resources from countries and redistribute them. Purchasing might be carried out locally or internationally. There are numerous ways to acquire goods, like buying them in bulk or keeping them at the vendor until needed. Utilising credit or readily available funds, procurement is conducted. In relief operations, procurement aims to make it possible for orders to be placed and delivered on time and for a reasonable price. To save delays and support the local economy, governments and organisations want to buy locally whenever possible. However, some businesses choose to stick with their trusted vendors in order to ensure the consistency and high quality of their goods or to negotiate a better price (Moeing & Mokhlesi, 2011).

5.12. The Transport and Execution System

For assistance to reach those in need at the appropriate time and location, transportation is essential. Global sourcing, drop shipping, military transport, commercial transport, non-commercial transport, third-party logistics companies, freight forwarders, charter planes, or even local transportation using automobiles, trucks, boats, planes, and even animals if necessary, are all possible (Moeing & Mokhlesi, 2011). However, the capacity of airports and ports following disasters, the state of the roads, and the cost of fuel all affect transportation. The types of vehicles that can be employed are determined by the accessibility to the disaster area and the distance to other urban areas that can offer assistance. The capacity along an access route, known as flow capacity, is a crucial factor in determining the time for the aid to reach the victims.

Transportation options could include military equipment, government vehicles, volunteers, and partners from the business sector. One of the most important activities and frequently the most expensive step in the logistics process is freight transit, which involves the movement of products from one location to another. Through the creation of place and time utility, freight transportation enhances the logistics process. There are four main forms of transportation: air, land, water, and rail. The two kinds of surface transportation – land and water may be further separated into modes of transportation that can be identified by the physical right-of-way (or fixed route the mode must take) and the technology on which they are dependent.

5.13. Modes of Transportation Optimised for Humanitarian Logistics: Air Cargo Supply Chain

The fastest and most expensive form of transportation for cargo is air. As a result, it is utilised in times of crisis or in the global supply chain for expensive items. Since express and parcel services like those provided by DHL or UPS primarily use specialised air and land transport networks and facilities, general air cargo needs to be distinguished from these services. On the other hand, the supply chain for air cargo involves several parties: the forwarders gather the shipments from the shipper and combine them at local warehouses across the continent. They choose the export airport and transport it there to gather all shipments in their air cargo hub-warehouse in accordance with the selected flight. The shipments by aeroplane are delivered to the handling agents, who then load air cargo containers or assemble air cargo pallets using local truckers. The planes are loaded with the containers or pallets that are brought to the runway.

5.14. Management of Transportation Systems

Research and publications on the advantages of information sharing in supply chain management are important for deriving the benefits of digitisation, in addition to the processes that are special to air freight. The majority of the papers explore the consequences of demand changes and the costs that ensue, with an emphasis on a traditional supply chain and the interaction of supplier, producer, and distributor (Barros et al., 2015; Marinagi et al., 2015; Rached et al., 2015; Schulze, 2009). In very similar and comparable ways, Elbert and Walter (2014) study the 'Exchange of information in the maritime transport chain analysis of process performance in the data flow of capacity utilization'. Based on this paper, elements of empirical investigations were applied to air cargo. The relationships between partners in the supply chain (forwarders, carriers, and other logistics service providers) were the subject of a publication only in Elbert and Walter (2014). Most often, simulation models and computations were used to quantify use, and only infrequently were empirical analyses linked to this process. A business planning policy, such, for instance, a mutually optimal order- and production policy, can be defined in ways of reducing the sum of total costs from customer and producer, according to SCM-theory-based techniques (Sucky, 2004).

5.15. Operational Bottlenecks

Loading ramps are regarded as a transportation logistics bottleneck both in theory and in practice. In this regard, numerous recent studies with a practical focus demonstrate that friction losses occur at the processing interfaces (Semmann, 2012). The site running businesses, in this case Handling Agents, strive for maximum ramp capacity and a steady flow of freight (Semmann, 2012). The goal of ramp management techniques is to maximise the use of the ramps. Efficiency losses result from the active management's frequent failure to take into account all boundary circumstances in practice. These losses, which are discussed in a special study by the federal office for freight transport, are not only complained about in practice but also have a significant impact on the daily planning of the site operating and cargo carrying enterprises (Semmann, 2012).

5.16. Tracking and Tracing

A forward process called tracking is used to identify the route that aid takes from its source to its destination. To find out where the shipment was shipped, tracing is a process that is done in reverse. The relief chain lacks a well-developed tracking and tracing system. In actuality, Excel is typically used for tracking. Logistics for disaster relief do not especially benefit from tracing. It is critical to be aware of what has been promised, ordered, coming soon, and already delivered. Receiving, customs clearance, shipping to intermediate facilities, and distribution are all made more difficult as a result of the lack of insight into inbound shipments at each stage of the supply chain. In actuality, the aim of delivery to the right people, at the right place, and at the right time is connected to tracking and tracing. These procedures are also necessary to demonstrate impartiality and neutrality in humanitarian activities (Moeing & Mokhlesi, 2011).

5.17. Stock Asset Management

Stock may build up throughout the relief chain. Collection locations can serve as warehouses, transshipment locations, and locations for preparation and packaging of goods. They may be found there or close to ports, airports, or border crossings. Stock asset management is the process of setting up warehouses at particular locations and setting up the supplies kept there for distribution. Warehouses and transshipment terminals should be strategically placed to make the best use of the infrastructure that is already in place while ensuring the safety of the assets and people. Warehouse preparation typically takes place during the response phase. Following the earthquake, Haiti had only two major storage facilities. These were situated close to the airport and on the grounds of the presidential residence. Transporting the aid to the populace in need proved to be incredibly challenging once it reached these locations. At this point, supplies need to be secured to prevent theft and spoiling, notification of the delivery of the products should be sent, and records of incoming supplies need to be kept. It is important to inspect loads to make sure they match the shipping papers and are not contaminated. Reverse logistics are used in the event that the items are polluted. The items must be destroyed, returned, or given to cattle.

5.18. Extended Point of Delivery and Relief to Beneficiaries

An inland location close to the affected area that can keep products until final aid distribution to recipients in order to meet relief supply chain objectives is referred to as an extended delivery point. The majority of relief efforts bring goods close to the refugee camps for storage. Food aid is regularly sent to camps by relief organisations, where it is prepared as needed and distributed. Points of delivery are selected by taking into account the distance to beneficiaries, the accessibility of assets after a disaster, and the state of the infrastructure at the time.

To put it another way, it is frequently challenging to effectively and safely distribute aid to the appropriate individuals and organisations. When supplies are exchanged between foreign and local organisations, there is a chance that they will end up on the black market rather than where they are needed. This emphasises the necessity of numerous stock asset management points. Delivery was quite difficult in the first week after the catastrophe. In an effort to circumvent the difficulties of getting supplies to people on the ground, food and water started being airdropped to the victims four or five days after the accident. (Moeing & Mokhlesi, 2011). However, as was already indicated, this resulted in some riots and bloodshed as people fought for the required aids. The distribution method was altered as a result, and aid convoys had to travel with security escorts; nevertheless, distribution was anticipated to return to normal with the arrival of additional aid, troops, and humanitarian workers.

The goal of humanitarian logistics is to provide aid to disaster victims. This aid must be dispersed in a way that is culturally suitable to people who actually require it and in proportion to their needs. Monitoring is required throughout the supply distribution process as well as throughout the storage phase to guarantee that these conditions are met. They take care to make sure that those that are more vulnerable get their fair portion of the food distribution. Distribution through identity cards or providing food for the family to female household heads are two examples of this (Moeing & Mokhlesi, 2011).

5.19. The Relief Supply Chain Umbrella: Coordination, Collaboration, and Communication

The administration of transportation, supply chain approaches for humanitarian logistics, education and training, resource management, partnership with the military, logistics information system, assessment of damage, acting in accordance with local and regional, decisive command and control, and competition for uncertain positions are only a few of the goals and objectives driving coordination, collaboration, and communication among the organisations participating in natural disaster responses.

It is crucial that those involved in the humanitarian effort find a way to cooperate despite what may appear to be competing responsibilities in order to offer relief in a complementary and effective manner. Without it, there will undoubtedly be duplication of effort in some areas and complete omission in others. Due to this, some segments of the affected people would feel more abandoned, which would hinder the overall relief effort (Moeing & Mokhlesi, 2011).

5.20. References

Arminas, D. (2005). Supply lessons of tsunami aid. *Supply Management, 10(*2), 14.

Byman, D., Lesser, I., Pirnie, B., Benard, C., & Waxman, M. (2000). Strengthening the Partnership: Improving Military Coordination with Relief Agencies and Allies in Humanitarian Operations, Rand, Washington, DC.

Chaikin, D. (2003). Towards improved logistics: challenges and questions for logisticians and managers. *Forced Migration Review, 18*. https://www.fmreview.org/logistics/chaikin

de Barros, A., & Ishikiriyama, C., & Peres, R., & Gomes, C. F. (2015). Processes and Benefits of the Application of Information Technology in Supply Chain Management: An Analysis of the Literature. *Procedia Computer Science, 55*, 698–705. 10.1016/j.procs.2015.07.077.

Elbert, R., & Walter, F. (2014). Information flow along the maritime transport chain - A simulation based approach to determine impacts of estimated time of arrival messages on the capacity utilization. In *Proceedings of the Winter Simulation Conference 2014*, Savannah, GA, USA, pp. 1795–1806, doi: 10.1109/WSC.2014.7020028.

Fritz Institute. (2005). Logistics and the effective delivery of humanitarian relief, Retrieved August 23, 2021, from http://www.fritzins titute.org/PDFs/Programs/tsunamiLogistics0605.pdf.

Khan, H., Vasilescu, L. G., & Khan, A. (2008). Disaster management cycle – A theoretical approach. *Journal of Management and Marketing, 6*(1), 43–50.

Marinagi, C., Trivellas, P., & Reklitis, P. (2015). Information quality and supply chain performance: The mediating role of information sharing, procedia. *Social and Behavioral Sciences, 175*, 473–479. https://doi.org/10.1016/j.sbspro.2015.01.1225

Moeiny, E., & Mokhlesi, J. (2011) Management of Relief Supply Chain & Humanitarian Aids Logistics through Supply Chain Resilience: Case Study: South West Asia Tsunami (2004). University of Boras School of Engineering. http://www.diva-portal.org/smash/get/diva2:1308842/FULLTEXT01.pdf.

Rached, M., Bahroun, Z., Campagne. J.-P. (2015). Assessing the value of information sharing and its impact on the performance of the various partners in supply chains. *Computers & Industrial Engineering*, *88*, 237–253. https://doi.org/10.1016/j.cie.2015.07.007.

Schulze, L., & Li, L. (2009). A Logistics network model for postponement supply chain. *IAENG International Journal of Applied Mathematics*, *39*, 2. https://www.iaeng.org/IJAM/issues_v39/issue_2/IJAM_39_2_03.pdf

Semmann, C. (2012). "Eiszeit an der Rampe". In *DVZ* (pp. 1–2).

Sucky, E. (2004). Coordinated order and production policies in supply chains. *OR Spectrum*, *26*, 493–520. https://doi.org/10.1007/s00291-004-0178-2

Chapter 6

Modelling Humanitarian Supply Chains

6.1. Introduction

Recently, supply chain configuration has drawn more and more interest from researchers and practitioners alike. Even though this topic is widely understood and well-explained technically in the literature that is currently available, it still presents challenges in reality, particularly when it comes to coping with real-life complexity, service level restrictions, and data mapping. We created our integrated approach in order to close these gaps. The use of computer simulation in logistics has various advantages from a management and research standpoint. For instance, it is possible to assess the impact of particular decisions before making them, and it is possible to simplify complex systems for easier comprehension. However, there are other issues with logistics simulation, including the possibility that the models are too sophisticated for management use, that there is little similarity between the model and the actual system, and that the simulation model has limited analytical capabilities.

Any simulation model designed for analysis in business situations should meet certain criteria. A possible list of such criteria includes the following:

(1) The minimal data entry.
(2) Data entry is simple.
(3) Simplicity of updating.
(4) Usability.
(5) Simplicity of comprehension.
(6) Minimal outside assistance.
(7) Lowest price for a PC.
(8) Quick response.
(9) A portable software suite (hardware compatibility).
(10) Create models of various corporate systems.

The computer model's usability is addressed by the first eight criteria. The final six criteria focus on how adaptable it is to different business scenarios. The Graphical Evaluation and Review Technique (GERT) is one computer simulation

Supply Networks in Developing Countries:
Sustainable and Humanitarian Logistics in Growing Consumer Markets, 69–78
Copyright © 2023 by Tatenda Talent Chingono and Charles Mbohwa
Published under exclusive licence by Emerald Publishing Limited
doi:10.1108/978-1-80117-194-620231006

technique that appears to be well adapted to logistical problems and fits most of the aforementioned criteria. Despite having a long history of management applications, GERT has never been used in the field of logistics.

Using GIS and Operations Research (OR) methods, Weigel and Cao (1999) addressed issues with technician dispatching and home delivery at Sears, Roebuck and Company. To manage its delivery and home service fleets more effectively, Sears used a geographic information system-based vehicle routing and scheduling system. Despite the fact that the issues at hand can be modelled as vehicle routing problems with time windows (Solomon, 1987), the scale, and, consequently, practical complexity of the issues at hand make them of interest from both a theoretical and practical standpoint. The authors created a number of algorithms, including one to create the origin and destination matrix, another to allocate resources, and finally algorithms to carry out sequencing and route improvement. The deployment of Sears technicians and home delivery services were enhanced by the integration of GIS and OR methods. It (i) decreased driving times by 6%; (ii) raised the number of service orders per day that each technician performed by 3%; (iii) decreased overtime by 15%; (iv) assisted in the reduction of routing offices from 46 to 22; and (v) generated a $9 million yearly savings. The effectiveness of this application also pointed to a potentially fruitful relationship between GIS and OR methods. It also assisted ESRI, the project's GIS consultant, in the development of ArcLogistics, a low-cost PC-based routing and scheduling program that offers top-notch capability to small businesses that previously couldn't afford it.

6.2. Existing Models: Linear Sequence Models Versus Cyclical Models

Disaster relief operations must take logistics into account while planning, purchasing, transporting, storing, tracking, and tracing supplies. The simplest disaster relief model shows a continuous progression of pre-event, disaster, and post-event, as Kelly (1998) underlined. Using this as a foundation, the now widely accepted conception of the National Governors Association (1979) proposes a four-stage standard process model for disaster assistance, which entails preparedness, response, recovery, and mitigation. Similar to Tatham and Kovács (2007), Ludema and Roos (2000, cited in Tatham & Kovács, 2007) define emergency, elementary (or subsistence), rehabilitation, and development relief as phases of disaster relief operations; preparation may be an extra step (Kovács & Spens, 2007). Although they might have some elements, linear conceptualisations of disaster relief are still being critiqued (see Kelly, 1998), which is why additional cyclical models have been created (Anderson, 1985; Carter, 1991; Cuny, 1985; Safran, 2003).

6.3. A Theoretical Model of Disaster Relief: Dual-cycle Model

A dual-cycle model of disaster relief activities serves as the foundation for the theoretical model, which will be discussed next. A stage of emergency response is followed by a stage of rehabilitation and reconstruction in the model, which depicts the operational responses to disasters and their recovery. On the other side, it includes tactical steps for anticipating and preventing disasters, like the mitigation and preparation phases.

The model shows that stages are not mutually exclusive within each individual cycle, but rather that overlaps are frequent. For distinct population segments, various stages – and actions within these stages – may even occur at the same time, and some relief efforts are relevant to more than one stage (Haas et al., 1977; Neal, 1997). The stages are interconnected, which allows them to function concurrently; they are not autonomous entities, with one halting and the next coming after (Hogg, 1980; Shaluf, 2008). For instance, mitigation and reconstruction initiatives are frequently carried out concurrently and, in theory, should be designed concurrently, but not always by the same players. Similar to this, because supply networks must be constructed swiftly, the associated stages of preparedness and disaster response may partially overlap. In reality, some disaster relief organisations concentrate almost solely on tactical planning and emergency relief activities, while others broaden their operational horizons or concentrate on long-term operations related to disaster region rehabilitation. By carefully utilising their amassed expertise and knowledge, these latter organisations likewise strive to lessen or prevent upcoming tragedies.

This model provides a unique and helpful portrayal of disaster relief operations that highlights the dual-cyclical character of these operations by highlighting the specific responsibilities of the disaster relief agencies. The model also offers a straightforward foundation for gaining a deeper comprehension of supply chain management (SCM) procedures in disaster relief operations. Before delving into the model, we take a look at the emergence of cross sector (between companies and relief agencies) and socially conscious partnerships in the disaster relief industry. These partnerships enable the transfer of best SCM practices from firms to relief agencies (Fig. 6.1).

6.4. Model-based Strategy for Simulation

A supply chain is the movement of goods, data, and services from the suppliers of raw materials via factories and warehouses to the final consumers. A supply chain consists of the businesses and procedures used to produce and distribute these goods, data, and services to the final consumer. The opportunities created by technological advancement are the primary factors behind supply chain management's growing popularity and use. Simulation is frequently used as a potent tool to address issues with supply chain logistics. However, because supply chain modelling incorporates multiple firms as opposed to modelling processes that are exclusive to a single organisation, it comes with extra challenges.

The expense of coordinating between the numerous independent suppliers in each supply chain and communicating with them has been a major impediment to complete supply chain management. When only one organisation is involved in the supply chain, creating a comprehensive model is not a challenge. When the chain crosses organisational boundaries, however, not many participant

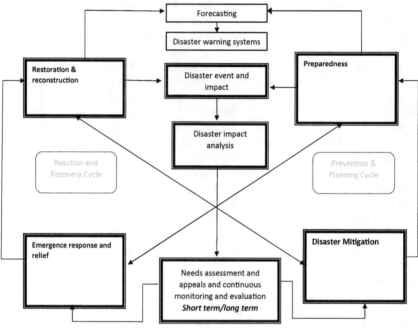

Fig. 6.1.   Model for Disaster Relief Activities.

organisations are open to sharing specific model information. Each organisation can create and construct its own simulation model to address this, encapsulating the internal data. In order to assess the simulated supply chain as a whole, it is therefore necessary to combine the independently designed and created simulation models. Because supply chain projects involving several firms often involve simulation coupling, there is a need for a well-designed common implementation framework for coupling the individual simulation models.

Reality can be interpreted by simulation as being composed of numerous systems that can be understood and controlled. 'A set of two or more interrelated elements of any kind' is the definition of a system. A system like this is represented by a model. In the sense that it is less complex than reality and may, thus, be more easily manipulated, a model is an abstraction of a system. A variety of options must be considered when making decisions if an organisation is to attain its objectives. Making decisions requires problem-solving, which is a necessary component of managing companies. In this view, managers are the ones who are in charge of solving problems, and they frequently do so by using a decision-making process (Fig. 6.2).

Finding the weak rings that make the supply chain as a whole or a portion of it vulnerable by studying its structure is crucial. Finding these weak areas is especially important when dealing with the supply chain for humanitarian goods because any disruption in the process of helping the afflicted population may lead to more deaths or worsen the horrible outcomes. Finding the elements that make a system more susceptible to interruptions is crucial. The ability of those

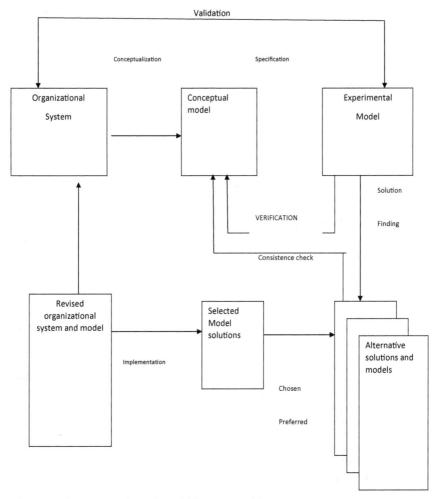

Fig. 6.2.   Supply Chain Vulnerability and Resilience.

chains to recover to their original or even superior form in the event of a disruption will be increased by eliminating or minimising those causes (Moeing & Mokhles, 2011).

6.5. Creating Supply Chain Resilience

In order to create a robust supply chain, Khan, Christopher and Burnes (2008) identifies four key concepts that must be followed. First, the supply chain needs to incorporate a large number of futures. The supply chain is better able to return to the previous stage if any unfavourable events occur thanks to these built-in futures. The second concept emphasises the need for teamwork in order to pinpoint the sources of risk. Finding the risk factors will enable removal of those factors or preparation for their effects (Moeing & Mokhles, 2011).

Another principle that Khan, Christopher and Burnes (2008) thought was essential for the supply chain's resilience is agility. A supply chain becomes more resilient the more swiftly it can respond to unforeseen circumstances. A system's risk management culture is also thought to contribute significantly to its resilience. It is critical to broaden our viewpoint and refrain from focusing solely on the supply chain when considering potential sources of risk. It is important to take into account that other supply chains or networks have a significant potential to introduce risk into our network.

6.6. Supply Chain Reconfiguration

Prior generations of supply chains were primarily focused on cost. However, the entities involved in the supply chain are required to adjust their perspectives and look into reengineering the network due to the expansion in risk exposure to businesses and the severity of the consequences. Focusing on a variety of elements can make it easier to achieve this goal.

6.7. Mapping the Supply Chain

It is important to see the supply chain as it should be in order to identify any weaknesses. After that, identifying the constraints and bottlenecks becomes more useful. Finding all the connections, nodes, and vital spots is essential. There are certain traits that put pressure on the supply chain. Long lead times, supplier monopolies, poor visibility, and links or nodes that are associated with high levels of risk are some examples of reasons that make it more important to reengineer a component of the supply chain.

6.8. Reconsidering Supply Approach for Humanitarian Logistics (HL)

Some businesses are likely to choose a single sourcing strategy for their supply since it can lower costs and make the quality control process easier. But it is important to realise that single sourcing makes the supply chain more exposed. The fact is that a balance between cost orientation and resiliency inclination must exist that taken into account by all the organisations that are going towards resiliency. Additionally, it is important to assess the suppliers' capacity for risk management as well as their preparations and plans for potential disruptions. To increase the supply chain's level of resilience, partners must be recruited who have a greater understanding of the risk management procedures.

6.9. Applying a Proper Supply Chain Strategy

The entities in the chain must not be constrained by supply chain strategy. Purely cost-driven supply chains may appear effective financially, but if there is a disruption, the resulting implications could be serious and result in significant expenses for them.

6.10. Collaboration in Supply Chain Management

A supply chain is a group of connected companies that form a network in which it is anticipated that physical items and information will be transferred. In such networks, the majority of the entities are likely to concentrate on the movement of products. But the point is that it is important to foster an environment in which all the entities voluntarily share the information and necessary data that helps the other partners to see more advancements in order to be able to mitigate risk, confront market fluctuation, and meet new requests wherever they arise.

The term 'knowledge chain' is a novel idea that tends to emphasise the importance of information as a key competency that a chain must possess. The culture behind it, which demands visibility and has a tendency to share critical and precise facts, is focused on constructing a knowledge chain. The process of experiencing them, documenting them, recalling them in the event that the same event occurs, and so on.

6.11. Agility

Returning to its capacity to adapt quickly to new changes, a supply chain's agility. The visibility and velocity of the supply chain must be taken into account when creating one. As was previously mentioned, the supply chain will be more apparent the better the information is shared. Time and distance both affect velocity. It is essential to cut the duration in half to boost the chain's velocity. There are three basic methods for dealing with time reduction.

In the beginning, various procedures were simplified and switched from series to more parallel ones. The best supply source, suppliers that can adjust to changes in volume and kind of requirements, and synchronising the planes with the aid of shared information are then required to achieve a reduction in lead time. Finally, get rid of non-value-adding procedures by doing away with those that don't offer anything that customers will be willing to pay for.

6.12. Creating a New Culture

It is necessary to establish a culture of risk management throughout the entire network, not just within the company. One of the elements that might validate the need for establishing this culture and hasten the process must be the role of leadership. A supply chain risk assessment is also necessary to identify the weak points in the network. Finally, the company needs a risk management time to regularly update the supply chain risk data.

A susceptible supply chain can exacerbate the effects of a natural or man-made disaster and raise the chance of losing more lives; hence, the elements listed above must be prioritised as essential when constructing or enhancing supply systems. Even after dealing with calamities of any kind, the procedure must be handled carefully. But even at this point, supply transformation managers still face a number of challenges.

6.13. Relief Supply Chain Management Challenges

It has been noted that the world population is rapidly increasing, there is a greater concentration of assets (and people) in high-risk areas, and there is growing social and economic interdependence. As a result, more than half of the 20 most expensive disasters on Earth have occurred since 1970. Natural catastrophes are becoming more frequent and more severe as a result of these tendencies coming together (Moeing & Mokhles, 2011).

The relief supply chain management team's primary problem after a disaster is how to quickly get the appropriate quantity of resources to the disaster area to meet the immediate demands of survivors. The following list of management problems is designed to highlight some of the key areas where supply chains for disaster assistance face management difficulties and offer potential areas for future management research and study.

6.14. Coordination and Cooperation Issues

The United Nations plays a major leadership role in international coordination, collaboration, and specified processes in the event of disasters, but without local government decision and request, no international action may be taken. In fact, in the event of a significant international calamity, the role and primary duty of the government (at the national/state/provincial/local/tribal levels) must be acknowledged. Even when permission is granted, there are still a few rare instances of power struggles and delays in decision-making because of distance, barriers to communication, or miscommunication.

6.15. Supply Chain Structure

To adapt and anticipate it over the various wants of the clients (survivors) and relief chain team members, some special arrangements and trims on the supply chain format are required. Depending on the intensity, location, type, accessibility of possible participants, anticipated needs, and established protocols, specific groups are involved in each disaster. As a result, the membership of the relief group could shift from one crisis to another, adding another level of complexity to the coordination. For instance, cargo security is a major concern while providing aid in various parts of the world. Other places can have little options for logistics because of tense interstate relations. Some highly qualified groups might not be allowed to enter or travel through certain countries, though.

6.16. Humanitarian Logistics and Relief Supply Chain Steps

There are some crucial actions that should be taken during the disaster response operation under the humanitarian logistics and relief supply chain umbrella, taking into account the number of organisations, workers, and relief items arriving on the ground and concerning the struggle to coordinate relief efforts in order to reach out effectively to those in need (Atasu & Van Wassenhove, 2008).

6.17. Conclusions

Natural disasters are occurring more frequently in Southern Africa, which has led to an increase in the number of disaster operations by humanitarian organisations (Lukamba, 2010). The effects of these events range from worsened hardship in the impacted community to fatalities. In light of this, humanitarian organisations must enhance their supply chain management procedures in order to increase the timeliness and effectiveness of their disaster response efforts.

There are two promising areas for future investigation. The first step is to further develop the structural configurations of the supply chain into a standardised framework for measuring sustainability performance. Performance evaluation is an essential component of sustainability's core work that can either considerably advance sustainable development goal (SDG) research or impede its lack thereof. In fields including ethical investing, ecological economics, and product engineering, advancements have been made. However, there isn't yet an interdisciplinary framework in place to compile the knowledge. Future research must locate and incorporate these currently dispersed findings into a generic framework that is theoretically sound and managerially applicable. The initial structural arrangement of the supply chain might be used as a starting point in this regard. In order to ensure interdisciplinarity, breadth should take precedence over depth and generality over specialisation in the early stages of such study. To combat the abstract aspect of sustainability and assure its operationality, it is also required to first adopt 'divergent thinking' before moving towards 'convergent action'.

Testing the suggested sustainable humanitarian Supply Chain (HSC) techniques in real-world settings is the second path for future research. This study is based on extensive fieldwork and is driven by the design science methodology. The recommendations would, however, benefit from intensive field testing to see whether they could be implemented and to enhance their operational quality. The research can be used to build HSCs that don't heavily rely on practitioners' cognitive abilities and value judgements during complicated and dynamic emergency responses, but instead make sustainable solutions the default choices.

6.18. References

Anderson, M. (1985). A reconceptualization of the linkages between disasters and development. *Disasters*, 9(1), 46–51.

Carter, N. (1991). *Disaster management: A disaster manager's handbook*. ADB.

Cassidy, W. (2003). A logistics lifeline. *Traffic World*, October 27, p. 1.

Cuny, F. (1985). What has to be done to increase the effectiveness of disaster interventions. *Disasters*, 9(1), 27–28.

Haas, J., Kates, R., & Bowden, M. (1977). *Reconstruction following disaster*. MIT Press.

Hogg, S. (1980). Reconstruction following seismic disaster in Venzone, Friuli. *Disasters, 4*(2), 173–185.

Holland, K. (2007). A new corporate path to disaster relief. *The New York Times,* December 23.

Kelly, C. (1998). Simplifying disasters: Developing a model for complex non-linear events. *Australian Journal of Emergency Management, 14*(1), 25–27.

Khan, O., Christopher, M., & Burnes, B. (2008). The impact of product design on supply chain risk: a case study. *International Journal of Physical Distribution & Logistics Management,* 38(5), 412–432. https://doi.org/10.1108/09600030810882834

Kovács, G., & Spens, K. M. (2007). Humanitarian logistics in disaster relief operations. *International Journal of Physical Distribution & Logistics Management, 37*(2), 99–114.

Ludema, M., & Roos, H. (2000). Military and civil logistic support of humanitarian relief operations. *Proceedings of the 10th international council on systems engineering annual international symposium,* July 16–20, Minneapolis, MN.

Lukamba, M. T. (2010). Natural disasters in African countries: what can we learn about them? *The Journal for Transdisciplinary Research in Southern Africa,* 6(2). https://doi.org/10.4102/td.v6i2.266

Moeiny, E., & Mokhlesi, J. (2011). *Management of Relief Supply Chain & Humanitarian Aids through Supply Chain Resilience.* Master Thesis. University College of Boras, School of Engineering.

National Governors Association. (1979). *Emergency preparedness project.* DCPA.

Neal, D. (1997). Reconsidering the phases of disaster. *International Journal of Mass Emergencies and Disasters, 15*(2), 239–264.

Safran, P. (2003). A strategic approach for disaster and emergency assistance. Proceedings of the 5th Asian Disaster Reduction Center International Meeting and the 2nd UN-ISDR Asian Meeting, January 15–17, Kobe.

Shaluf, I. (2008). Technological disaster stages and management. *Disaster Prevention and Management, 17*(1), 114–126.

Solomon, M. (1987). Algorithms for the Vehicle Routing and Scheduling Problem with time Window Constraints. *Operations Research, 35,* 254–265. http://dx.doi.org/10.1287/opre.35.2.254

Tatham, P., & Kovács, G. (2007). An initial investigation into the application of the military sea-basing concept to the provision of immediate relief in a rapid onset disaster. *Proceedings of the productions and operations management systems 18th annual conference,* May 4–7, Dallas, TX.

Weigel, D., & Cao, B. (1999). Applying GIS and OR Techniques to Solve Sears Technician-Dispatching and Home Delivery Problems. *Interfaces, 29,* 112–130. https://doi.org/10.1287/inte.29.1.112

Chapter 7

Strategies and Opportunities for Reverse Logistics

7.1. Introduction

The chapter defines and discusses reverse logistics as a critical area for supply chains. Opportunities and strategies are identified and recommended for various humanitarian logistics operations for closed loop environmentally friendly operations. Reverse logistics, which primarily targets plastics and glass materials, is often recognised as a more environmentally acceptable method of recovering garbage for recycling and reuse. Some businesses utilise incentives to encourage customers to reuse or return product containers and worn, damaged, or unwanted goods when creating their products and managing their reverse logistics (Ferri et al., 2014; Santos et al., 2014). People have also been inspired to participate in reverse logistics for environmental preservation and to stop the ongoing loss of the earth's resources, according to Fehr et al. (2010). Due to weak waste management legislation, these approaches have mostly become popular in the industrialised world, with limited acceptance in the developing world.

Reverse logistics handles trash by utilizing the three pillars of reuse, recycling, and proper disposal. Carter and Ellram (1998) claim reverse logistics can be considered as a way for businesses to become more sustainable. Recycling is one of the best methods for controlling waste because it primarily lowers the amount of garbage produced while also giving otherwise useless materials a marketable use (Matter et al., 2013; Troschinetze & Minelic, 2009). Reusing materials includes recycling, which is defined as returning waste to the manufacturing line in order to lower production costs and provide new opportunities. Recycling fundamentally involves bringing lost or discarded objects back into the manufacturing cycle in order to conserve energy and natural resources (Dias & Braga Junior, 2016). As a result, it has grown to be a significant source of potential for recycling businesses to lower supply chain costs while enhancing visibility and profitability as well as the lifespan of their products (Chiou et al., 2012; Frota-Neto et al., 2008).

Wong (2010) emphasises the expanding potential importance of reverse logistics in city logistics improvements and modelling targeted at lowering congestion,

Supply Networks in Developing Countries:
Sustainable and Humanitarian Logistics in Growing Consumer Markets, 79–88
Copyright © 2023 by Tatenda Talent Chingono and Charles Mbohwa
Published under exclusive licence by Emerald Publishing Limited
doi:10.1108/978-1-80117-194-620231007

resource conservation, emissions reduction, and recycling in logistical activities. As a result, businesses are now concerned about the trash that results from their post-consumer products, whose return needs to be taken into account so that they might use reverse logistics to create a commercial opportunity. Another beneficial result is that small enterprises that recycle, reuse, and resell can be formed.

The specialty and focus of reverse logistics is the enhancement of a product's value. It helps maximise the use of resources while preserving the environment. Reverse logistics is a popular practice among businesses since it is environmentally friendly and promotes social responsibility. The past 50 years, which started in the 1950s boom years and ended in the 2000s recession, have given rise to a new range of products and items from the conventional supply chain. These products include those that are broken but repairable, out-of-date, unsold items on store shelves, recovered items, and accessories. The development of formal systems for value recovery and appropriate disposal has been directed by South African government rules for the storage, maintenance, transport, and disposal of manufacturing process residuals. It is essential to place more of an emphasis on reverse logistics and logistics, concentrating on the use of computer technology, sophisticated office automation, and constrained application to sectors that assist military and military systems. The ongoing ratification of green laws and the escalation of environmental concerns have greatly influenced numerous logistics and sustainability choices (Chiou et al., 2012).

Bioenergy products like biogas, bioethanol, and biodiesel can be made from recyclable garbage, general organic waste, and biomass. The anaerobic enzyme biogas can be utilised as a supplement or as a natural gas substitute at the electrical and thermal power plant. Contrary to fossil fuel systems, photosynthesis has only lately begun to incorporate carbon dioxide, which is produced during the creation and combustion of biogas. As long as plants continue to absorb carbon dioxide, these emissions do not result in a net generation of carbon dioxide, leaving the atmosphere neutral. In order to sidestep the food and energy issue, biodiesel is typically produced from used vegetable oils, while bioethanol is typically produced from the leftover sugarcane after it has been converted to sugar (Bauer et al., 2007).

The complete process of collecting and moving trash to specific locations for value addition, mostly into bioenergy, is the main focus of this research. The life cycle analysis methodology was used in this study since it is the only one that can be used to calculate the value and effects of the entire process. As a result, the environmental impact of the substrate supply, the bioenergy production process, the energy input and source for the digestive process, infrastructure, labour, and direct emissions from the process all affect the overall environmental performance of bioenergy production. Berglund and Börjesson (2005) discussed the use of digests. Due to the varied energy components in different biomasses, which can be utilised in anaerobic digestion, varying amounts of bio-semen are produced. Farmers frequently purchase or cultivate high energy crops to increase biogas output, and these frequently raise the issue of food versus energy. As a result, this study promotes the utilisation of leftovers or trash from human consumption and use in the production of bioenergy.

There are two types of logistics throughout the life cycle of any product: forward and reverse. When we talk about forward logistics, we mean the supply chain from production to distribution. Reverse logistics refers to the aftermarket supply line that efficiently transports product returns back to the manufacturer. It also refers to the supporting function that logistics plays in the products, such as waste disposal, source reduction, recycling, material substitution, and reuse. Consequently, reverse logistics is a component of a larger returns management process (Pienaar & Vogt, 2012). It is possible to think of logistics' supporting function in the returns management process as both physically moving and positioning returned goods and analytically analysing logistical data to increase effectiveness and efficiency.

7.2. Returns Management Is About

Avoidance: This refers to evaluating returns, figuring out why products are being returned, and putting programmes in place to reduce the amount of return requests.
Gatekeeping: The initial stage of the reverse flow involves screening return requests and the returned goods. To make the reverse flow efficient, logistics should contribute to the formulation of the gatekeeping policies and possibly be involved in their implementation.
Disposition: There are many options, including recycling, remanufacturing, renovating, and disposing of in landfills.

Management of product returns and waste disposal make up the majority of product returns management. Waste must be effectively and responsibly reused, recycled, or disposed of as it is an inevitable byproduct of manufacturing activity. Some actions related to returns management are:

- Customer service and help desk inquiries.
- Gatekeeping (managing the insertion of products into the reverse chain).
- Depot repair services.
- Management of recycling initiatives.
- Accounting and reconciliation procedures related to returns.
- Physical logistics activities involved in moving and positioning returned/ disposed material.

7.3. Product Recovery and Waste Management

The removal and disposal of trash produced during the production, distribution, and packaging operations are also included in reverse logistics. The waste hierarchy's ranking of waste disposal choices according to their effects on the environment is depicted in Fig. 7.1. Waste disposal options can be divided into four categories: cleaner procedures, recycling, treatment, and disposal.

The best course of action is to minimise or prevent creating waste in the first place.

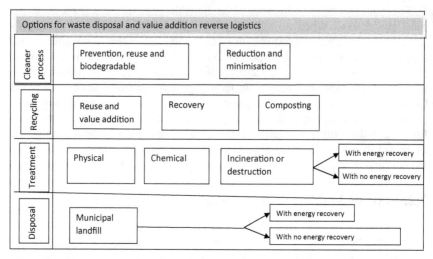

Fig. 7.1.   Waste Hierarchy Chronology.

7.4. The Impacts of Reverse Logistics

The environment for reverse logistics is quite different from that of forward logistics. Forward logistics plans the best distribution of a small number of products from one or more manufacturing or warehouse points to numerous distribution or retail points based on sales and marketing forecasts. Reverse logistics, on the other hand, is more responsive and involves more obvious product flows. Only consumer or downstream channel members' actions can trigger a response or reaction from an organisation. In reverse logistics, there is typically no precise forecasting plan for the expected volume of activities.

7.5. Cost Implications

Although the reverse logistics system is a cost centre, these expenses are incurred to help the organisation meet specific goals and are related to the following activities:

(1) *Location of the product (investment and running costs)*: Most of it is from the disaster area where relief was donated.
(2) *Transportation*: The majority of it came from the disaster's epicentre, where relief was donated. Primarily involves the transportation of unused supplies, vehicles, and other stationary items for repurposing or in the event of future disasters.
(3) Product assortment.
(4) *Disposal*: Primarily landfill or incineration of obsolete materials and packaging.
(5) Recycling, reusing, repairing, upgrading, and remanufacturing.
(6) *Documentation*: For tracking and tracing products as they enter, leave, and move through the system.

7.6. Barriers to Good Reverse Logistics

(1) *Legal issues*: Most governments in emerging economies demand proper paper-work for returned products. This is a highly labourious and time-consuming process, and failure to comply could result in legal action being taken against the company.
(2) Reverse goods are viewed as 'junk' by many organisations in the developing world, who don't want to waste their resources on them.
(3) The products are viewed as being unworthy of investment because the majority of enterprises lack the tools or resources to add value to them.

7.7. Logistics and the Environment

The logistics function directly affects the environment since it uses resources and demands energy. As a result, a logistics manager must consider environmental concerns like recycling, energy saving, and carbon footprints.

Consumers are putting more and more pressure on businesses to run sustainably. Customers anticipate businesses to follow the law, protect the environment, and use resources responsibly.

The degree to which supply chain activities adhere to the overall set of criteria that a company sees as being important to its stakeholders is referred to as 'environmentally sound'. Environmental considerations, for example, have a greater impact on many logistics decisions; many products can no longer be disposed of in landfills; businesses are required to take-back their products when they reach the end of their useful lives; and the availability and cost of landfills are decreasing.

Strategies which an organisation can follow to reduce its carbon footprint include:

(1) Utilise renewable energy sources, such as wind or solar energy, to actively endeavour to lower the carbon footprint by redesigning products or changing the way services are offered.
(2) Reduce energy use during production.
(3) Create structures that make the most of natural light and collect rainwater.
(4) Make an effort to buy local items.

7.8. GSCM Compliance-centred Strategies for Reverse Logistics

Organisations typically use compliance-based tactics in response to environmental regulations. Instead of a collaborative, integrated supply chain, this typically leads to more unintentional supply channels. Most often, this occurs when the product is simple and standard and there is little internal participation. Reverse logistics can be green, but they are not the same as green supply chains. Companies that want to integrate green technologies into their supply chains frequently employ these tactics (Agrawal et al., 2015). Government and industry laws, the development of global quality systems like ISO 14000, the application of performance standards, and the procurement of contracts for suppliers to satisfy particular regulatory criteria are some of these initiatives. Use broad supplier or purchasing rules, similar to the primary certification systems.

An approach focused on compliance has the following advantages:

- Benefits of environmental performance.
- Application of a system that is well recognised.
- Third-party performance management.

These elements raise market, interest group, government, consumer, and supplier awareness and acceptance. These techniques have the drawback of being responsive, but their competitive advantage is constrained due to a lack of innovation, customisation, and simple duplication across rival supply chains. The system only ensures adherence to legal standards because it is run in a weakly collaborative context. Therefore, innovation and the economy have limited further advantages (Frota et al., 2008).

7.9. Agile and Lean-based Strategies for Reverse Logistics

Supply chains must first be lean, eliminating any waste, and then agile, responding to environmental changes, if they are to be effective and efficient. After the Japanese Toyota manufacturing operations' principles were applied, lean tactics emerged and became increasingly popular. These tactics concentrate on eco-efficiency depending on the effectiveness of goals within the company. Waste management and collection are two examples of green measures that might yield additional benefits.

The supply chain can be extended with performance standards to maximise economic performance, cut waste and resource consumption, and provide environmental performance thanks to the lean strategy, which blends environmental performance with operational efficiency. Businesses can use green business practices to promote goods that reduce waste production, conserve resources, and protect the environment (Chiou et al., 2012). Lean strategies have the advantages of promoting eco-efficiency throughout the supply chain and easily integrating with the organisation's existing optimisation and cost-cutting objectives. Direct strategies, on the other hand, do not support ground-breaking environmental management techniques like sustainable product design, innovation, and material exchange. Lean manufacturing is regarded as being technically unsound and needs to be supplemented by an agile strategy.

7.10. Innovation-centred Strategies for Reverse Logistics

To support changes in environmental rules, innovation-driven strategies concentrate on the creation of specialised technology, product designs, procedures, and strict environmental performance requirements. Focusing on a more ecologically focused performance approach in recovering and shipping end-of-life items serves as the foundation for innovation-driven strategies, which differ from lean manufacturing-driven strategies. Therefore, the supply chain's primary investment focus is on sophisticated performance criteria for resource recovery as well as on specialised procedures and technology (Dias & Braga Junior, 2016). Given that the business is still in its infancy, there are a variety of entrepreneurial opportunities that can be established.

7.11. The Future: Closed Loop Strategies

These tactics seek to close the loop by integrating forward and reverse logistics. The goal of this study is to identify the waste's reverse logistics and attempt to connect them to the customer's forward logistics and renewable bioenergy. Throughout the supply chain, high levels of innovation and entrepreneurship are required. Businesses also need to integrate, collaborate, and establish industrial symbiosis so that one organisation's waste can be used as a raw material by another. According to Badenhorst (2016), businesses must create this strategy from the beginning of the design process. This study will demonstrate how these collaborations can occur between organisations that are already well-established. Closing the loop is about recapturing value either for reuse or recycling or remanufacture. Materials need to be recovered and transported to collaborative organisations that will recapture value of end-of-life goods, returned products, post-use, and damaged and decayed organic matter. This tends to increase the environmental performance of the entire supply chain. Ways to control and optimise reverse logistics still need to be fully explored as visibility and forecasting still lacks immensely (Badenhorst, 2016).

The goal of closed loop techniques is to combine environmental and economic performance. Closed loop techniques can also have unfavourable societal effects, particularly when take-back, reuse, and reverse logistics are involved. These can be challenging to understand and process in a useful way. Infrastructure for closed loop techniques may exacerbate problems because they might be expensive or perhaps require completely new production systems that can work with the returned material. Members of the organisation and the community could be opposed to the move. Some people simply may not support bioenergy, recycling, and reuse. Some even go so far as to claim that there is no such thing as climate change and choose to use fossil fuels even in the face of alternative renewable bioenergy being made available (Dutta et al., 2016). The study will attempt to address these concerns of resistance and discover strategies for educating, integrating, and involving the entire community in some decision-making. The energy sector offers few opportunities for complete loop chains because recovered garbage is typically transformed into a brand-new product that will be burned to provide energy, which might be seen as just promoting the zero-waste component.

When forward and reverse supply chain operations are merged into a single system in order to include returned goods back into the production or distribution network, closed loop supply chains are created. In essence, it is a supply chain that produces zero waste, meaning that all resources are reused, repurposed, or composted. The phrase is also used to describe corporate take-back programmes, in which things are given back to the maker after serving their purpose.

7.12. Reverse Logistics and the Environment

More often than not, decisions involving reverse logistics are influenced by environmental factors. Due to capacity issues, many products can no longer be disposed of in landfills, and these products are also losing favour because they are temporary fixes that also contaminate the environment with toxic gas emissions. When deciding on environmental policies and regulations, it is important to consider the environmental impact of the procedures involved in transporting garbage from one enterprise to another for value addition. Due to their assistance in managing and clearing waste, enabling proper disposal, bioenergy production, incineration, and other value-adding processes, reverse logistics have a significant positive impact on a healthier and cleaner environment. Companies may be required to take-back their goods when they reach the end of their useful lives, improving the environment, and cutting down on landfill usage.

Reverse logistics is a strategic variable that many businesses must decide to emphasise in order to get a competitive edge. If executed properly, including reverse logistics policy into company strategy can be advantageous to an organisation. Reverse logistics capabilities can also help businesses earn points for good corporate behaviour when they employ them for charitable purposes like philanthropy. With the community in which they are also located, they can create opportunities, and mutually beneficial relationships. Since they also draw labour and other resources from the region in which they are located, these can be mutually advantageous.

7.13. Challenges for Reverse Logistics

(1) Establishing a cooperative relationship to achieve mutually beneficial outcomes.
(2) Inefficiencies, a lack of expertise, and inadequate support systems that increase the processing time for returns.
(3) Reverse logistics efficiency and activity measurement is still relatively difficult, which makes management difficult because visibility is typically low.
(4) Large amounts of returns inventory leading to higher inventory holding costs in the warehouse; unknown total costs of the returns process; uncertainty of policies (government regulations or pressure from environmental agents); increased production and population usage, which causes returns to arrive faster than processing and landfilling, leading to an increase in illegal dumping.
(5) Reducing the amount of time it takes to decide what to do with returned goods once they arrive; many products can no longer be dumped in a landfill; decrease in landfill availability and increase in landfill costs; management inattention and the lack of importance of reverse logistics.

7.14. Conclusions

The majority of reverse logistics operations involve shutting down businesses following a calamity. The idea of backward logistics differs greatly from that of forward logistics. Forward logistics plans the best distribution of a small number of products from one or more manufacturing or warehouse points to numerous distribution or retail points based on sales and marketing forecasts. Reverse logistics, on the other hand, is more responsive and involves more obvious product flows. Only consumer or downstream channel members' actions can trigger a response or reaction from an organisation. There is typically no clear forecasting plan for the volume of reverse logistics activities that can be anticipated, which makes it difficult to maximise transportation system economies of scale and predict production of bioenergy.

7.15. References

Agrawal, S., Singh, R. K., & Murtaza, Q. (2015). A literature review and perspectives in reverse logistics. *Resources, Conservation and Recycling, 97*, 76–92.

Badenhorst, A. (2016). Prioritising the implementation of practices to overcome operational barriers in reverse logistics. *Journal of Transport and Supply Chain Management, 10*(1), a240.

Bauer, A., Mayr, H., Hopfner-Sixt, K., & Amon, T. (2009). Detailed monitoring of two biogas plants and mechanical solid–liquid separation of fermentation residues. *Journal of Biotechnology, 142*, 56–63.

Berglund, M., & Börjesson, P. (2006). Assessment of energy performance in the life-cycle of biogas production. *Biomass Bioener. 30*(3), 254–266. 10.1016/j.biombioe.2005.11.011.

Carter, C. R., & Ellram, L. M. (1998). Reverse logistics: A review of the literature and framework for future investigation. *Journal of Business Logistics, 19*(1), 85–102.

Chiou, C. Y., Chen, H. C., Cheng, Y. T., & Chung, Y. C. (2012). Consideration factors of reverse logistics implementation—A case study of Taiwan's electronics industry. *Procedia – Social and Behavioral Sciences, 40*, 375–381.

Dias, K. T., & Braga Junior, S. S. (2016). The use of reverse logistics for waste management in a Brazilian grocery retailer. *Waste Management & Research, 34*(1), 22–29.

Dutta, A., Schaidle, J. A., Humbird, D. et al. (2016). Conceptual Process Design and Techno-Economic Assessment of Ex Situ Catalytic Fast Pyrolysis of Biomass: A Fixed Bed Reactor Implementation Scenario for Future Feasibility. *Top Catal, 59*, 2–18. https://doi.org/10.1007/s11244-015-0500-z

Fehr, M., de Castro, M. S. V., dos Reis Calçado, M. (2010). Condominium waste management by private initiative: A report of a 10-year project in Brazil. *Waste Management & Research 28*, 309–314.

Ferri, G. L, Chaves Gde, L., & Ribeiro, G. M. (2015). Reverse logistics network for municipal solid waste management: The inclusion of waste pickers as a Brazilian legal requirement. *Waste Manag., 40*, 173–91. doi: 10.1016/j.wasman.2015.02.036.

Frota, L. (2008). Securing decent work and living conditions in low-income urban settlements by linking social protection and local development: A review of case studies, *Habitat International, 32*(2), 203–222. https://doi.org/10.1016/j.habitaint.2007.08.016

Matter, A., Dietschi, M., & Zurbruegg, C. (2013).Improving the informal recycling sector through segregation of waste in the household – the case of Dhaka Bangladesh. *Habitat Int. 38*, 150–156.

Pienaar W. J., & Vogt J. J. (2012). *Business logistics management : A value chain perspective* (4th ed.). Oxford University Press.

Quariguasi Frota Neto, J., Bloemhof-Ruwaard, J. M., van Nunen, J. A. E. E., & van Heck, E. (2008). Designing and evaluating sustainable logistics networks. *International Journal of Production Economics*, *111*(2), 195–208. https://doi.org/10.1016/j.ijpe.2006.10.014

Santos, R. B. M., Braga Junior, S. S., Silva, D., & Satolo, E. G. (2014). Analysis of the economic and environmental benefits through the reverse logistics for retail. *American Journal of Environmental Protection*, *3*, 138–143.

Troschinetz, M. A., Minhelcic, R. J. (2009). Sustainable recycling of municipal solid waste in developing countries. *Waste Management*, *29*, 915–923.

Wong, C. (2010). *A Study of Plastic Recycling Supply Chain*. Research Paper. The Chartered Institute of Logistics and Transport UK.

Chapter 8

Information Technology in Humanitarian Logistics

8.1. Introduction

Information technology's (IT) influence and significance on humanitarian logistics are examined. The research results and trends in the area of IT in humanitarian logistics will also be reviewed in this chapter. IT makes the supply chain more transparent and visible. Aims to find and buy the appropriate goods and supplies at the appropriate moment, and to deliver them at the appropriate location, at the appropriate time, in the appropriate quality, and for the appropriate price. All parties involved – from the donor to the beneficiary – are more effective as a result of IT. IT has many advantages, some of which are visibility into the supply chain, tracking and tracing of relief supplies, and inter-agency cooperation. Additionally, it aids in proactive decision-making and optimum choice selection. Organisations must choose whether to create or purchase information systems. Creating your own internal information systems has advantages such as personalisation and perhaps lower expenses. High maintenance expenses, the necessity for ongoing updates, and the requirement for specialist employees are drawbacks.

Researchers like Clark and Culkin (2007), Thomas and Kopzack (2005), Van Wassenhove (2006), Kleindorfer and Van Wassenhove (2004), Tomasini and Van Wassenhove (2009), Thompson, and others have focused on trying to implement and introduce humanitarian logistics and supply chain management to humanitarian organisations (2008). Others recommend networks for Africa to promote the realisation of the Millennium Development Goals and Supply Chain Analytics for Humanitarian Logistics Transformation, which also emphasises the critical role of humanitarian logistics.

8.2. Research Constructs

The various methods that businesses utilise IT for supply chain management (SCM) are referred to as types of IT use in SCM. Three distinct IT uses in SCM transaction processing, supply chain planning and cooperation, and order

Supply Networks in Developing Countries:
Sustainable and Humanitarian Logistics in Growing Consumer Markets, 89–98
Copyright © 2023 by Tatenda Talent Chingono and Charles Mbohwa
Published under exclusive licence by Emerald Publishing Limited
doi:10.1108/978-1-80117-194-620231008

tracking and delivery coordination were discovered and selected as the first construct based on the earlier research mentioned above. Transaction processing, the first category of IT use, refers to the use of IT to speed up routine information transfers between supply chain parties. Information is often shared in this sort of IT use in relation to processes including order processing, billing, delivery verification, creating and sending dispatch advices, and creating order quotes. The second category of IT use, supply chain planning and collaboration, involves using IT to share planning-related data, such as demand projections and other demand information, inventory data, and production capacity data, with the goal of enhancing supply chain effectiveness. The monitoring of individual orders or shipments, which may include components or finished goods, with the goal of coordinating their delivery or providing timely information about their position, constitutes the third type of IT use in SCM (Chingono & Mbohwa, 2016).

8.3. Technological Shortage

The creation and management of information systems, IT, and logistic systems are all hampered by action-focused cultures, tacit knowledge, financial challenges, and a disregard for SCM standards. Although investing in more advanced SCM systems could eventually lead to cheaper costs and more effective operations, agencies do not have enough people and financial resources to do so. Many points in the supply chain are difficult or impossible to acquire information since the majority of NGOs lack an effective electronic infrastructure (Lee & Zbinden, 2003). For instance, most disaster relief organisations use Excel for tracking and switch from electronic systems to paper early in the handling process (Gustavsson, 2003), which causes them to have limited visibility into incoming shipments. This change in practice makes it more difficult to complete tasks like receiving, customs clearance, shipping to intermediate warehouses, and distribution along the supply chain (Russel, 2005). Additionally, it seems that few field participants make an effort to evaluate and specify specific technological needs and strategic SCM shortages, or to promote the creation and application of technological solutions (Ratliff, 2007). Thus, it becomes necessary to build specialised, adaptive technological solutions in order to meet the distinct requirements of the intricate supply chain processes involved in disaster relief operations (Thomas & Kopczak, 2005).

8.4. Usage Level of IT

When properly connected and used, IT provide relief organisations with powerful tactical and strategic tools that can significantly advance and strengthen their competitiveness (Porter, 2001). IT is used to streamline communication, information exchange, and/or knowledge sharing among the various departments that make up the relief organisation. As a result of removing obstacles to effective real-time communication and information sharing, IT serves as an aid to networking among employees, beneficiaries, and partners (Scott, 2001).

Through the merging of new technology with society and reaction, IT aids humanitarian organisations in innovating, enabling the generation of new knowledge and scientific discovery (Brownson, Diem & Grabauskas, 2007). Relief organisations use IT to boost productivity, communication, employee motivation, reaction time, and enhance operational dynamics (Sternberg, Hagen, Paganelli & Lumsden, 2010). IT in the humanitarian sector has evolved into a tool that can alter the organisational structure of an industry as well as a way to process data and store contacts. According to Galliers (1994), relief organisations must fundamentally reevaluate their management of data and innovation assets with a view to achieving their primary goals because of the rapid pace of technological advancements and the impact of data innovation on the changing competitive environment.

Many authors and experts in the field of hierarchy agree that data innovation has a significant impact on how an organisation conducts its business (Frankfort-Nachmias & Nachmias, 1996). Applications for data innovation, for example, can be used to increase the organisational authority's proficiency level and the effectiveness of administrative tasks. These programs are also used as tools to make projects more organised and to provide managers with better information.

8.5. IT Applications for Relief Organisations

When it came to supporting evacuees and internally displaced people in the middle of 1998–1999, the effects of application coordination of IT help mediations were more significant than those that had already occurred in relief theatres, such as Somalia (1992–1993), Bosnia (1994–1955), and Rwanda (1994). This was a result of evolving IT machinery during the combination of electronic organisations emerging from the automated change that rose in the early to mid-1990s and manifested itself in the determination of the Internet as an information and particular mechanical assembly, regardless of your point of view. In order to access pooled relief information, interact slightly with on-the-ground workers (if permitted by the establishment), and broadly set help engagement boundaries, this IT transaction progress involved aid groups. As a result, customary assistance procedures and systems underwent amazing alteration (Davis & Fugate, 2012).

The development of an electronic data medium, specifically the web and the World Wide Web, and its subsequent widespread use by both corporate and private effort opened up new possible outcomes anywhere information recovery and cover or intra-correspondence between organisations and personnel were performed through traditional methods (visits to libraries, letters, redesigns, and so on). Online collaboration among jewellery should be possible throughout the globe sooner than it has previously been possible using traditional postal mail, phones, faxes, cables, and organisations.

It was never again necessary to take wires or faxes to business partners for communication (like a mail 13 station). The transmission was enabled via the PC and modem over the internet (Gorry, 2008).

The web's recent development gave employees the ability to look up information and use the medium's intriguing features (Dess et al., 2014). Relief organisations found themselves in this environment while planning and implementing the assistance intervention. From the analysis of the selected crises, it appears that IT application gathering and coordination were done formatively and using a hybrid strategy of crucial masterminding and hands-on training. Development applications which have been aided by central office boundaries, for instance, the Internet, have step by step divided down to help handle operations (Lindenberg & Bryant, 2011).

8.6. Effectiveness of IT on Relief Logistics

Harrison and Hoek (2008) claim that a wide range of operations take place within a relief organisation when it comes to logistics. IT enhances the flow of data among various units in a generally beneficial manner, improving the viability of the coordination in store network, transportation, and various units during disaster operations. Data innovation improves needs assessment by ensuring that the field staff is aware of the supplies that are currently in stock, sharing arrangements of provisions including costs and lead times to enable program staff to plan their procurement activities better, keeping staff informed of procurement activities to foster a better understanding of the processes and foster trust, and also providing more precise data to the budget holders to prevent under-or over-spending. Additionally, the systems give warehouse inventory data to program supplies to make sure that the supplies are used properly and to enable more precise division of logistics overhead costs across the various programs and program budgets.

IT solutions, according to Sople (2007), help improve logistics decision-making, provide information on costs, increase control over the physical distribution and relief supply of goods and services, improve accounting, link data and systems with supplier systems, and help access the performance of key logistics functions like the percentage of on-time supplier deliveries, the cost of operating warehouses, or the overall logistics spend (Blecken & Hellingrath, 2008).

The Fritz Institute, which led the development of Helios Software, claims that the program can offer a number of advantages (Howden, 2009). By providing tactical relief supply visibility from mobilisation to warehouse, it maximises the impact of relief efforts. By offering new viewpoints on a common source of information, it also increases the efficiency of relief supply operations, improving coordination across all organisational working units.

Thevenaz and Resodihardjo (2010) claims that the use of IT enables strategic perceivability from each of these points of view by automating coordination forms at both the home office and field levels. By enabling customers to track donations as they move through the entire manufacturing network, IT also strengthens the bond between aid organisations and donors. Organisations obtain precise information about the majority of their gifts, from business to unselfish products and endeavours. It gives organisations the opportunity to screen and write about donations, improve donor communications, and more deeply engage donors in the work of the organisation. It also increases the perceivability of help supply from the perspective of the giver (Oso & Onen, 2009).

8.7. Drivers for IT Use in SCM

The second element, drivers for utilising IT in SCM, refers to the justifications for using IT in SCM in a particular way. Based on our review of the literature, we predicted that the case companies would use IT in transaction processing for the reasons listed below: lowering operational process costs (manual labor), enhancing information quality by removing human error, and accelerating information transfer between organisations. We also proposed that the number of transactions is a driving factor in the use of IT for transaction processing. Furthermore, it was presumed that information about supply chain coordination is exchanged, particularly in corporate situations that are unstable, unexpected, and logistically challenging. Finally, we anticipated that project-oriented businesses and situations with in-transit delivery consolidation would execute tracking and coordinating operations.

8.8. Forecasting and Quantification

Generally, the AIDS and TB Unit, with cooperation from Natpharm, forecasts and quantifies national HIV/AIDS commodities (Zimbabwe). The final quantities to order and the cash available for procurement typically drive it. Since there is no organised method for predicting national commodity requirements, this is

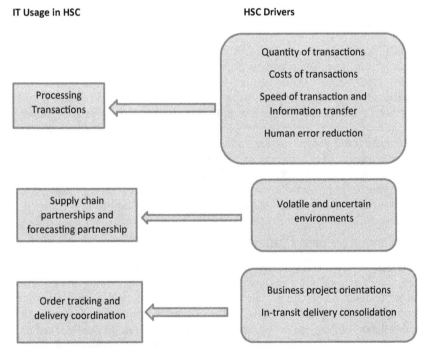

Fig. 8.1.　Relationship Between IT in Supply Chain Management and the Drivers for Using It.

mostly inaccurate. The establishment by the government of a clear, long-lasting, systematic mechanism for estimating and measuring the needs for national commodities is supported. Only when crucial logistics information on the supplies provided to victims is collected and reported on a regular basis will projections become better and more accurate.

8.9. Procurement

The survey indicates that the facilities' resupply amounts are computed digitally. Currently, the majority of donors are importing HIV & AIDS supplies using their own procurement processes. Due to the lack of coordination, there is a risk of overlap and gaps in the availability of certain commodities. The central coordination of procurement through information sharing between various NGOs, the government, and donor organisations is crucial. The National ARVs program or the already established Procurement and Logistics Subcommittee might be used to promote information exchange in this manner. Commodity procurement should always be integrated into the pipeline with other operational components of the logistics system, such as forecasting and quantification, inventory management, and calculating stock status. More funding should be made available to organisations so that the risks and chances of stock outs and defaults are reduced. Since the availability of funds was primarily what drove procurement, this is important (Takang et al., 2006).

8.10. Transaction Processing

The majority of businesses used IT to handle business with their suppliers. Additionally, they processed transactions with their customers using IT. In the businesses, these were primarily utilised for processing orders and invoices. IT was occasionally utilised to process dispatch advices and delivery verifications. The usage of IT for transaction processing was found to be driven, as anticipated, by the reduction of manual effort and costs, improvement of information quality, accelerated information transfer, and volume of transactions. Furthermore, most of the organisations shared the same motivations for employing IT for transaction processing. To cut costs connected with human work involved in sales transactions and to improve the accuracy and speed of information exchange between businesses, the corporations sought to eliminate manual labour.

8.11. Supply Chain Planning and Collaboration

In the study, there was less use of IT for supply chain planning and collaboration than there was for transaction processing. Additionally, this is in line with earlier research on the dissemination of planning data (Kauremaa et al., 2004; Kemppainen & Vepsäläinen, 2003). IT was employed for supply chain planning and collaboration by less than half of the organisations. Additionally, contrary to what was expected, the case companies' unpredictable and logistically challenging environments did not stand out as a driver for this type of IT use. The information shared through the IT system was instead used for carrying out a specific cross-organisational process, which was a significant point of commonality among the majority of the companies using IT for supply chain planning and collaboration.

8.12. Order Tracking and Delivery Coordination

The majority of the organisations in the survey employed IT systems to track orders, coordinate the progress of delivery, and provide this information. Of these, order-specific progress reports were manually updated into an extranet website upon request from relevant parties.

8.13. Summary and Conclusions on HSC and IT

Considering the ideas that have been developed and previous studies, it is clear that the adoption variables must be taken into account for IT to be successful within a company. As examined by Blecken and Hellingrath (2008), Kreidler (2013), Kovács and Spens (2014), and others, some of these essential considerations include the type of technology, users of the technology, context of technology adoption, and expected outcomes of employing technology (2011). This justification led to the selection of the variables under investigation in this study as key determinants in disaster relief operations, namely the effectiveness of IT and challenges on the implementation of effective IT in relief logistics.

The effective coordination between the relief groups, the impacted individuals, and the stakeholders engaged was made possible by the use of IT. Increased automation, adaptability, information flow, and the link between resource planning and response are the causes of the coordination. The study finds that the effectiveness of relief logistics will rise if all independent variables are maintained at zero. On the same day, there was no statistically significant correlation between IT use and relief logistics. The efficiency of relief logistics is correlated with IT use. This reinforces the idea that effective use of IT and relief logistics go hand in hand. This is a strong correlation, therefore an increase in IT utilisation indicates improved relief logistics.

8.14. Recommendations on Information Technology and the Way Forward

The three categories of IT use in this study – transaction processing, supply chain planning and collaboration, and order tracking and delivery coordination – were used to analyse the use of IT for SCM, as detailed in Figure 8.1. Additionally, the motivations for these various IT usage types were looked at. The three IT use categories that have been suggested accurately reflect the roles that IT plays in SCM based on the empirical data that was gathered for this study. The categorisation not only clarifies this hotly debated subject but also offers a framework for future study on the application of IT in SCM. The drivers for the transaction processing role of IT in SCM were found to be as expected: reduction of manual effort and expenses, improvement of information quality, accelerated information transfer, and volume of transactions. Additionally, it was discovered that this IT use is motivated by the ongoing nature of the commercial relationship. It was discovered that the adoption of cross-organisational processes, most frequently the vendor managed inventory (VMI) system, is what drives the usage of IT in supply chain planning and coordination. An additional motivator for this use of IT was the unpredictable and logistically challenging environment. Finally, it was discovered that the usage of IT for order tracking and delivery coordination was driven by business project orientation and in-transit consolidation. Additionally, this usage of IT was primarily necessitated by the requirement to coordinate additional tasks or deliveries dependent on the status of particular tracked supplies. Study on various supply chain coordination techniques should be conducted in addition to research on the use of IT in supply chain management in order to better comprehend the complex phenomenon of supply chain management. Humanitarian missions are difficult to evaluate in terms of success. In the world of private enterprise, financial success is the benchmark for performance. This analysis is more complicated for non-profit organisations because it takes into account both more manageable factors like cash flow and harder to define ones like unmet need. The extreme urgency and tempo of these types of activities make it difficult to maintain complete track, control, and accountability of the humanitarian initiatives and their results, and there is typically little time for analysis and recording.

To successfully and efficiently increase the organisations' profile, stay current with industry developments and legislation, manage and organise data more easily, accurately track their finances, safely maintain their clients' contact information, understand who is using their services and how they can expand their reach, enable benefit clients to support one another through online groups, save money, and more.

8.15. References

Blecken, A., & Hellingrath, B. (2008). Supply Chain Management Software for Humanitarian Operations: Review and Assessment of Current Tools, 5th International ISCRAM Conference, Washington, DC, USA.

Brownson, R.C., Diem, G., Grabauskas, V., et al. (2007). Training practitioners in evidence-based chronic disease prevention for global health. *Promotion & Education*, 14(3), 159–163. doi: 10.1177/175797590701400305

Chingono, T., & Mbohwa, C. (2016). Social and environmental impact for sustainable bio-gas production by the city of Johannesburg. Proceedings of the 2016 International Conference on Industrial Engineering and Operations Management Detroit, Michigan, USA, September 23–25.

Clark, A., & Culkin, B. (2007). A Network Transshipment Model for planning humanitarian relief operations after a natural disaster. Paper presented at EURO XXII – 22nd European conference on operational research, Prague.

Dess, G. G., Lumpkin, G. T., & Eisner, A. B. (2014). Strategic management: Text and cases. McGraw-Hill Education.

Frankfort-Nachmias, C., & Nachmias, D. (1996). *Research Methods in the Social Sciences*, Fifth Edition. Arnold.

Fugate, B. S., Autry, C. W., Davis-Sramek, B., Germain, R. N. (2012). Does knowledge management facilitate logistics-based differentiation? the effect of global manufacturing reach. *International Journal of Production Economics*, *139*(2), 496–509. https://doi.org/10.1016/j.ijpe.2012.05.008.

Galliers, R. D. (1994). Strategic information systems planning: myths, reality and guidelines for successful implementation. In R. D. Galliers & S. H. Baker (Eds.), *Strategic Information Management* (pp. 129–147). Butterworth–Heinemann, Oxford.

Gorry, G. A. (2008). Sharing knowledge in the public sector: Two case studies. *Knowledge Management Research & Practice*, *6*(2), 105–111, doi: 10.1057/palgrave.kmrp.8500172

Gustavsson, L. (2003). Humanitarian logistics: context and challenges. *Forced Migration Review*, *18*, 6–8.

Harrison, A., & Hoek, R. I. V. (2008). *Logistics Management & Strategy: Competing Through the Supply Chain*. Pearson College Div: London.

Howden, M. (2009). How Humanitarian Logistics Information Systems Can Improve Humanitarian Supply Chains: A View from the Field. In J. Landgren & S. Jul (Eds.), *Proceedings of the 6th International ISCRAM Conference*, May 2009, Gothenburg, Sweden.

Kemppainen, K., & Vepsäläinen, A. P. J. (2003). Trends in industrial supply chains and networks. *International Journal of Physical Distribution & Logistics Management*, *33*(8), 701–719.

Kleindorfer, P. R., & Van Wassenhove, L. N. (2004). Managing risk in global supply chains. In H. Gatignon & J. R. Kimberley (Eds.), *Strategies for building successful global businesses* (pp. 288–305, chapter 12). Cambridge University Press.

Kovács, G., & Spens, K. M. (2007). *Humanitarian logistics in disaster relief operations*. Emerald.

Lee, H & Zbinden, Marc. (2003). Marrying logistics and technology for effective relief. *Forced Migration Review*, *18*.

Lindenberg, M., & Bryant, C. (2001). *Going Global Transforming Relief and Development NGOs*. Kumarian Press.

Oso, Y., & Onen, D. (2009). *Writing Research Proposal and Report*. Nairobi: Jomo Kenyatta Foundation.

Porter, M. (2001). Strategy and the Internet. *Harvard Business Review*. *79*, 62–78, 164.

Russell, T. E. (2005). The Humanitarian Relief Supply Chain: Analysis of the 2004 South East Asia Earthquake and Tsunami. Thesis, Georgia Institute of Technology, https://dspace.mit.edu/handle/1721.1/33352.

Scott, W. R. (2001). *Institutions and Organizations*. Sage Publications.

Sternberg, H., Hagen, A., Paganelli, P., & Lumsden, K. (2010), Intelligent cargo - enabling future's sustainable and accountable transportation system. *World Journal of Science, Technology and Sustainable Development*, *7*(3), 253–262. https://doi.org/10.1108/20425945201000016

Takang, E., Dragana, V., Celestine, K., & Nyeriwa, J. (2006, May). *Management of HIV and AIDS commodities in Zimbabwe—A capacity assessment of NatPharm and Ministry of Health and Child Welfare*. DELIVER, for the U.S. Agency for International Development.

Thevenaz, C., & Resodihardjo, S. (2010). All the best laid plans conditions impeding proper emergency response. *International Journal of Production Economics*, *126*(1), 7–21.

Thomas, A., & Kopczak, L. (2005). *From logistics to supply chain management: The path forward in the humanitarian sector*. Technical report. Fritz Institute.

Thompson, P. M. (2008). Supply chain analytics for humanitarian logistics transformation. Humanitarian logistics: Network for Africa Rockefeller Foundation Bellagio Center *conference*, May 7, Bellagio.

Tomasini, R.M., & Van Wassenhove, L. N. (2004). Pan-American health organisations humanitarian supply management system: Depoliticization of the humanitarian supply chain by creating accountability. *Journal of the Public Procurement, 4*(3), 437–449.

Tomasini, R., & Van Wassenhove, L. N. (2009a). From preparedness to partnerships: Case study research on humanitarian logistics. *International Transactions in Operations Research, 16*, 549–559.

Van Wassenhove, L. N. (2006). Humanitarian aid logistics: Supply chain management at high gear. *Journal of the Operational Research Society, 57*, 475–489.

Chapter 9

Humanitarian Logistics in the Industry 4.0

9.1. Introduction

The chapter focusses on defining Industry 4.0 and identifying opportunities and challenges. The chapter also discusses the concept of the connected factory in Industry 4.0 and how it can be applied in humanitarian logistics. The Industry 4.0 is bringing about significant changes in society and industry, as well as in the pace and outlook of the economy, the organisation of work, how human–machine interactions should be oriented, and other areas. However, the capability to accurately understand and perceive these shifts will allow us to increase our awareness and ability to track and read the markets, which will encourage organisational adherence to this paradigm shift pattern. As a result, the acquired sensibility will enhance how consumers choose products and services, decide between buying and renting, and interpret the emergence of new paradigms like the shared economy, collaborative innovation, additive manufacturing, social networks, and digital platforms, among others, that are accelerating the pace of change. Information and communication technologies (ICT) use and evolution in industry have become inescapable during the past 10 years, largely due to how important they are to boosting organisational effectiveness and level of competitiveness. This has accelerated the use of ICT across most industry activities, but especially in the areas of logistics and production. Applications like enterprise resource planning, warehouse management systems, transportation management systems (TMS), and intelligent transportation systems (ITS), which are widely employed by most enterprises, serve as examples of this technological evolution. However, the real-time and on-demand information that can be obtained through VANET systems, sensor networks, drone points, and business intelligence systems will help management make decisions that are more quick and effective in the near future.

The logistics challenges in an industry Internet of Things (IoT) context may call for things like: a high need for transparency (supply chain visibility); integrity control (right products, at the right time, place, quantity, and condition, and at the right cost); dynamic 'reconfigurability' of supply networks, especially by

Supply Networks in Developing Countries:
Sustainable and Humanitarian Logistics in Growing Consumer Markets, 99–127
Copyright © 2023 by Tatenda Talent Chingono and Charles Mbohwa
Published under exclusive licence by Emerald Publishing Limited
doi:10.1108/978-1-80117-194-620231009

re-examining service-level agreements with upstream and contracted suppliers; and supply network design, towards achieving lean, agile, and flexible supply chains. The term 'Logistics 4.0' will be used to describe logistics in this setting. It is important to note that the goal of Logistics 4.0 from a technology and in-line processes standpoint is not to replace humans in their work, but rather to eliminate errors and have quicker processes where information can be communicated easily and in real time. People in charge of the processes and those who can take charge of any system failure will always be required. In this chapter, we want to concentrate the conversation on some of the major obstacles that must be overcome in order to satisfy the demands of the Logistics 4.0 age.

9.2. Science and Technology in Disaster Risk Reduction (DRR)

A key component of effective DRR in Africa is investment in science and technology. Science and technology are crucial for comprehending the intricate relationships between physical systems and people as well as the ripple effects of different dangers. Science and technology also offer chances to create remedies for regional social and economic problems.

Science and technology advancements in data quality and analysis could lead to better DRR measure creation and use. For instance, by bolstering disaster data infrastructure and scientific institutions and networks, risk assessment methodologies and the generation and dissemination of risk information into policy would be improved. One of these is the African Science and Technology Advisory Group (Af-STAG), which promotes systematic international and intranational learning. Securing sufficient levels of investment in science, technology, engineering, and math is one of the main problems facing many African nations. Current political will, financial limitations, and academic curricula do not support science and technology advancement. As a result, many African nations struggle to properly utilise scientific information for DRR.

At the national, regional, and continental levels, work should continue to improve the generation of risk information and promote the expansion of information management capabilities. Governments are urged to look for information sharing opportunities and consider the advantages of recent developments in data and information management. The implementation and oversight of the Programme of Action for the Implementation of the Sendai Framework in Africa can benefit greatly from multi-hazard and systemic risk assessment. To increase data collecting, monitoring, and evaluation systems, which in turn provides the evidence base for risk-informed decision-making, partnerships between institutions are crucial in this regard. The ultimate goal of risk knowledge generation is to educate and inspire stakeholders. To do this, risk assessment and the generation of risk information should develop messages that are logical, focussed, and intended to be effectively communicated. The continuous development of a scientific, technological, and ethical base for DRR and integration of sciences into both policy and practice for disaster risk management should be the main priorities for DRR.

9.3. Transportation Management Systems

A supply chain management (SCM) component with a focus on transportation logistics is a TMS. A TMS makes it possible for an order management system to communicate with a warehouse or a distribution centre. In order to manage and control rising freight costs, integrate TMS with other supply chain technologies (like global trade management systems and warehouse management systems), and handle electronic communications with clients, business partners, and carriers, TMS has evolved. TMS has grown to be a well-liked option for businesses of all sizes and in all industries as their breadth of offerings has expanded to include these and other capabilities. A TMS is unquestionably a crucial component of the Logistics 4.0 concept given the widespread use of IoT and the unavoidable path to Industry 4.0. For a logistical process to be more efficient and productive, logistics 4.0 leverages real-time and inline data. A TMS is necessary for a business to be able to monitor freight movement, negotiate with carriers, consolidate shipments, use the platform's advanced functionalities, and communicate with ITS. GPS technology can be used by a company to locate its own vehicles accurately while they are on the road. Every year, TMS functions increase, and it is anticipated that more businesses will embrace these systems in the near future in an effort to boost overall transportation management and customer service. Cloud-based TMS is starting to become the norm as cloud services and computing become more widely available. In order to substantially reduce the amount of on premise installs in the future, the most significant software companies are quickly migrating their TMS solutions to the cloud. TMS is changing business strategies because the most recent TMS provides better end-to-end supply chain visibility. Small- to medium-sized businesses are adopting TMS because it increases the upper end of return on investment, which is a result of the increased use of mobile devices and services. Applications for smartphones will be included into TMS solutions.

IoT and TMS will become more and more crucial in the logistics and transportation sectors. Transportation and logistics companies can track the movement of physical objects from an origin to a destination across the entire supply chain, including manufacturing, shipping, and distribution, as more and more physical objects are outfitted with bar codes, RFID tags, or sensors. Promising IoT solutions are also available to transform vehicle services and transportation infrastructure. IoT technology can be employed to improve car sensing, networking, communication, and data processing capabilities as well as share underutilised resources among vehicles in a parking lot or on the road. IoT technologies, for instance, enable the tracking of each vehicle's present location, monitoring of its motion, and forecasting of its future location. In the very near future, making the SCM more and more flexible and efficient through the use of an appropriately defined and configured TMS that interacts with IoT devices, or what we refer to as a 'Smart TMS', will be essential for achieving complete Logistics 4.0 operation.

Clever transportation systems: The cutting-edge discipline of ITS interacts with a wide range of domains, including transportation management, control, infrastructure, operations, policy, and control techniques. Virtual operations, planning strategies, sensor technologies, positioning systems, and data processing are just a few of the new technologies that are included into ITS. Being a global society, the ITS becomes a vital part of the world we live in. Virtual technology integration is a novel idea in the field of transportation and is crucial to solving issues in a worldwide society. ITSs are crucial for boosting security and dependability, speeding up travel, facilitating traffic, and lowering risks, accident rates, carbon emissions, and air pollution. A reliable platform for transportation is provided by an ITS. ITS has several uses, including electronic toll collection, highway data collection, TMS, vehicle data collection, transit signal priority, and emergency vehicle preemption. ITS can be deployed in navigation systems, air transport systems, water transport systems, and rail systems in addition to providing other services for vehicle traffic. Generation 4.0 of ITS uses multimodal systems that include personal mobile devices, vehicles, infrastructure, and information networks in addition to providing solutions for personal contextual mobility. The effectiveness of the fleet and the logistic process are supported and enhanced by ITS, which significantly enhances the outcomes for the transportation community in terms of sustainability and the economy.

An ITS will soon be able to improve the efficiency of logistics through the convergence of machine-to-machine communication and cooperative systems technologies, using real-time and in-line data collected through VANET systems, sensor networks, drone points, and business intelligence systems. This will improve the decision-making quality of management and become more flexible and efficient. Considering Logistics 4.0, a fully functional ITS environment can be used for: intelligent truck parking and delivery area management; multimodal cargo, that is, supporting planning and synchronisation between different transport modes during the various logistic operations; CO_2 footprint estimation and monitoring; priority and speed advice, that is, saving fuel, cutting emissions, and minimising the presence of heavy vehicles in urban areas; eco-drive support, that is, encouraging truck drivers to adopt more fuel- and CO_2-efficient driving practices.

Compared to the level of digitalisation across organisational boundaries, the level of digitalisation within transportation businesses is far higher. This fact implies that further work has to be done. However, as long as there is no financial incentive for the entire industry to work together in creating a shared communication infrastructure, this condition is unlikely to change. We outline our strategy for creating such an infrastructure in this chapter utilising the design science methodology. The objective is a decentralised, open web-based network run by transport organisations themselves. Using expert interviews as a foundation, it is contended that the current system creates frictions that our approach might assist eliminate, creating an incentive for participation. In order to provide an overview of the current implementation state, the proposed system is described in terms of its existing technological foundation, the web of needs (WoN), and the extensions required to provide the necessary functionality.

In recent years, businesses in the transportation industry have improved their IT infrastructure, making it easier for customers to access the services they offer. Users may create accounts, book transports, schedule pick-up and delivery times, and pay their bills with ease using mobile apps and websites. These changes lower the transaction costs associated with onboarding and becoming a new client. However, there are certain disadvantages to this method of digitalisation. For starters, creating and maintaining these tools comes at a significant cost. Because of this, they are primarily created to satisfy the needs of the transporter rather than its customers. Instead of allowing customers to quickly switch between suppliers and evaluate service offerings and costs among vendors, they prefer to lock users into a streamlined one-stop shop for transportation. Instead, customers are presented with a bewildering array of apps, online accounts, and communication channels, each of which only allows them to communicate with a single vendor.

Uber's and Airbnb's recent financial achievements (Airbnb, 2022; Uber, 2017) have demonstrated the necessity for a vendor-independent medium where supply and demand might collide. A platform like this for managing transactions between market players acts as a uniting force that encourages standard interfaces, lowers the cost of partner search, and fosters trust among newly discovered partners. Although it addresses some of the problems with the more conventional manner of digitisation, this method has flaws as well. Most notably, matchmaking platforms frequently produce situations where it's winner-take-all (or winner-take-most). It makes more sense for a participant to join the platform that already has more of the clients the participant is interested in for any given product or service. As a result, there are only a few powerful platforms with a de facto monopoly. The platform business model's inherent logic dictates that only transactions that are directly or indirectly beneficial for the platform should be permitted to take place. Since each participant manages their own infrastructure, the platform model enables participants to connect with a larger pool of potential partners than the traditional model, but it also places new restrictions on that pool due to the platform's own self-interest: only platform users are permitted to interact based on the following:

(1) *Trust.* Established relationships between the consignor and the transporter are extremely valuable, especially when the freight is of a significant volume or value. It is challenging to trust new participants, and it is not seen required once successful business connections have been established. Because players favour current business ties and do not need to be matched with new partners, this conclusion casts doubt on the applicability of our research. On the other side, it would encourage a feature that promotes confidence in new partners as well as one that allows one to represent and utilise their professional network.

(2) *Digitalised communication.* Only within companies is transportation digitalised, and even within organisations, the actual execution is frequently not digitalised (communication with driver or for confirming handovers). If it is digitalised between companies (as opposed to using email or messaging apps), it is set up such that the client company integrates the transport company's API or makes use of its user interface. Market participants believed that phone calls were the primary form of communication, with written confirmation sent via email. Companies do have systems in place to track their shipments using barcodes, matrix codes, or electronic identification

tokens, but they don't appear to be consistent among businesses. Because it demonstrates that there is space for automated communication across firms, this study supports the problem relevance.

(3)   *Documents.* It becomes more complicated when consignors and consignees require that the original paper paperwork from the consignor be given to the consignee. The CMR1 consignment note (UNECE, 1956) is one such document that must be signed by the consignee and returned to the consignor; failure to collect the signed CMR consignment note may result in significant fees. On the other hand, the consignee has little to no motive to return it, which can result in critical issues. This finding, along with Finding 2 (digitalised communication), provides compelling support for greater technical harmonisation of transport document standards and their smooth incorporation into daily operations. The UN Convention on the Contract for the International Carriage of Goods by Road, abbreviated as CMR, 2 Electronic data interchange has mostly replaced paper delivery paperwork. It should be noted that a number of European nations currently offer the digital e-CMR Waybill in relation to the CMR document (UNECE, 2008). But in none of our interviews did it come up.

(4)   *Privacy.* For those involved in the transportation industry, maintaining trade secrecy is a crucial concern. Many experts expressed fear that their contracts and bids would be scrutinised by other parties in an open system and as a result were quite wary of our work. Many experts said they would be in favour of the approach if requests for quotes and their bids could only be disclosed to a particular audience.

(5)   *Appointments.* The difficulty of scheduling pick-up and delivery appointments, as well as the effects of mistakes, can differ substantially depending on the mode of transportation and the circumstances surrounding the consignee. The telephone is the primary communication method for scheduling appointments and providing updates. Large logistics firms have specialised channels for communication (apps or automated SMS). This result generally supports the applicability of our work if the technology is able to integrate processes and tools for scheduling appointments in order to standardise the situation, relieve the burden of last-minute improvisation, and provide a trustworthy record of the events that led to a problem.

(6)   *Calls.* Some experts believe it's crucial to be able to speak with your counterpart in addition to writing. It facilitates speedy problem solving, aids in establishing trust quickly (video calls or in-person meetings even more so), and is a useful method of preserving the client connection. If possible, it would be possible to contact the appropriate person (e.g. call the truck driver to inform them of an important change). This study argues in favour of including audio or video chat in a system that manages transportation relationships. A conference call with several participants, according to one broker, would be perfect.

(7)   *Certificates.* Some experts claimed that having to demonstrate that every link in the logistics chain possesses a specific accreditation, such as the GMP+ certificate for sustainable production, causes friction. This result

confirms the significance of the problem and may encourage the adoption of blockchains.

(8) *Framework agreements.* Each transport assignment is not set up individually by high-frequency consignors. Instead, they establish a framework contract, choose their transportation partners, frequently on an annual basis, and then carry out a number of transports with quickly determined costs. This result appears to cast doubt on the problem's applicability because it disproves the requirement for a system that pairs up transportation partners for each individual transfer. The described situation, however, might even be improved if the solution makes it possible to find transportation partners for framework agreements and set up individual transports based on a framework agreement, possibly in a private call for proposals among partners with whom a framework contract has been established.

(9) *Return freight.* Because a freight for the return trip needs to be found, getting a transportation quote for a one-time transport can take a while (one week is not unusual for agricultural goods). This finding demonstrates the relevance of the problem, as the delay creates friction during the information or negotiation phase, which could be lessened by a quicker method of locating a transport request for the return trip. The ability to offer a transport only if a corresponding return contract can be found, and to automatically represent and monitor the condition satisfaction, would be a solution feature that could be particularly helpful in this situation.

(10) *Price sensitivity.* According to numerous experts, customers make their purchasing decisions mostly based on pricing when it comes to transportation. When it falls short of the expected standard, the quality of the service (respect for appointments, promptness and accuracy of responses, and absence of damages) only weighs negatively on the decision. A solution for matchmaking like the one we're putting forth certainly fills a demand from customers, but it does so at the expense of transporters, who appear to feel threatened by our idea.

(11) *Price negotiation.* Price bargaining, according to several professionals, is essential to the industry. A system that prohibits negotiation is unacceptable. This finding suggests a negotiating aspect but has no bearing on our assessment of the problem's importance.

(12) *Quality dimensions.* Due to price sensitivity, some experts claimed they would not want to compete globally with everyone but felt their product was of greater quality than alternatives that were more affordable. In order for customers to understand the increased price, open competition would need to be able to advertise verified quality measurements. This conclusion demonstrates the need for technology to enable the ability to distinguish between offerings in a number of aspects and to establish verifiable service/ offer quality claims. The deeper issue raised by this study is that, other from price, customers frequently are unaware of the aspects of quality they need, either because these needs are implicit or because customers lack expertise. Therefore, it would be helpful if the technology offered a way for initiating a conversation with the client regarding service quality with the purpose

of educating them about alternatives so they could make a more educated selection. This is in addition to offering a means for verifiable claims.

(13) *Wrong assumptions.* Important knowledge can occasionally only be found implicitly. For instance, the recipient of a shipment of agricultural products might only be able to unload a dumper truck, not any other kind of truck. However, the transporter is assuming that the recipient is aware of this fact, which could result in the use of the incorrect kind of truck, causing delays and additional costs at the time of delivery. This finding lends support for automatic information exchange that can automatically detect incompatibilities like the one above and is machine-interpretable, standards-based.

(14) *Freight exchanges.* Transporters are averse to using freight exchanges to acquire new assignments since the prices they may demand there are so low that it is actually more cost-effective to make an empty return trip than to obtain a contract there. As the technology may have a similar impact for transporters as a whole, this discovery can be interpreted as disconfirming the relevance of our research. However, it's probable that this impact is due to pricing-driven systems, in which case the quality dimensions may help to improve the situation for carriers.

(15) *Contract negotiation.* Although contract negotiations may not always be essential, when they are, they can be time-consuming and prone to mistakes. Sometimes one party just dictates the terms of the contract. This is the situation when transporters submit bids in pursuit of a transport partner for a longer-term business partnership or when a transport company offers standardised services together with standardised terms. Individual transport tasks occasionally require contracts to be set up, which is typically done using MS Word papers sent back and forth via email. One of our interview participants at least acknowledged the desire for a more effective integrated solution that would provide more clarity at this stage.

9.4. Humanitarian Logistics Knowledge Base

9.4.1. Web of Needs

The WoN technology is the key component of our approach (Kleedorfer et al., 2014). Fig. 9.1 shows how it functions in its entirety. Participants broadcast supply and demand in a machine-readable format on servers (WoN nodes) in a decentralised network (1a, 1b) so that they may be located by specialised, independent matching services (2) that find compatible (supply, demand) pairs and notify them by sending a hint message (3). The participants in charge of the supply and demand objects have the option of creating a channel of communication and exchanging messages.

The goal of WoN is to provide a framework for common interaction patterns while allowing for the development of domain-specific specialisations. WoN is entirely based on resource description framework (RDF) (Manola & Miller, 2004) as a data description language and the web as its basic framework: the entire data structure, consisting of supply and demand, their connections, and the complete

Decentarlisation	Verified	Immutable
Organised via effective P2P network	Through signatures and data mining	Through consensus algorithm

Fig. 9.1.   Basic Properties of Blockchain.

data exchange, are represented as linked data. This prevents a break from occurring between the framework and the content (i.e. RDF that can be accessed on the web, Bizer et al., 2009). By representing needs (supply or demand), rather than users, in the system, the participant's privacy is protected. Each need can have a unique cryptographic key pair that is used to verify any messages it sends. A hash produced from the previous message history is iteratively signed to automatically secure the integrity of the communication history (Kleedorfer, Panchenko, et al., 2016). With this method, two participants can use their communication channel as a shared RDF database to which they can both contribute data by sending messages, but they cannot edit or delete previously sent messages.

WoN discussions have the immutability quality, which at first appearance makes them resemble blockchain systems (Nakamoto, 2008). Because signatures can only be produced by discussion participants and the WoN nodes they utilise, the immutability property in WoN is not quite as reliable as it is in a well-known blockchain. As a result, the threat model and trust model in blockchain and WoN are very different from one another. However, it should be emphasised that WoN provides functionality on a different level than blockchains: expressing supply and demand, matching, and messaging are not concerns of blockchain systems; therefore, it remains to be seen whether trust and threat models in WoN are acceptable for practical applications. The observation that, in practice, the conversation that precedes a transaction must be interpreted as the contract both parties agree to in the absence of any more formally defined agreement is the basis for WoN's decision to include a cryptographically assured message history. Therefore, it's critical that they can rely on an unalterable message history to support their case in the event of a disagreement. It is sufficient to have each other's signatures on each message in order to accomplish this.

9.4.2. i-Cargo Ontologies

The European Union (EU) project i-Cargo, which was completed in 2015 (Garcia, 2015; Hofman et al., 2016), is a highly relevant research study that we may build upon. The development of an open freight management ecosystem encompassing several businesses and nations was one of the objectives of i-Cargo. The project produced a variety of artefacts that we can utilise in our work, chief among them a set of ontologies created especially for the transportation industry (Daniele & Ferreira Pires, 2013). These ontologies are the transport ontology, the logistics core ontology LogiCo (Daniele, 2013a), and the logistics services ontology LogiServ (Daniele, 2013b). (Daniele, 2013c). They serve as a foundation for using RDF to describe the entities pertinent to the transport domain. Such entities as consignor and consignee, modes of transportation, consignments and transported items, packing, delivery, and pick-up choices, transportation requests, and transport execution plans can all be described using these ontologies.

The name of our project, Open Logistics Networks, comes from the use and extension of WoN to support transportation and logistics. This offers a virtual environment in which any number of actual market participants can be represented in self-organised open networks. The overall concept is to place the relevant entities inside the needs using the WoN technique, to characterise them according to the LogiCo, LogiServ, and transport ontologies (or maybe according to simplified versions thereof), and to publish those needs on the web.

Domain-specific descriptions can be used by matching services for precise matching and to meet the needs of creating an RDF-based communication channel. Each of these connections naturally results in an RDF model that is accessible to both parties over HTTP. The set of RDF triples that define the needs and the triples exchanged in the communication channel make up this entity. In the event that any of these triples cite further sources, those sources are also included in the shared model. Take as an illustration a need that describes the transportation of a consignment of oil seed to an oil mill, as seen from the side of the oil mill, as inspired by false assumptions. It makes reference to an RDF description of the loading technology. The related need includes a connection to an RDF description of the vehicle and explains the delivery event as observed by the transporter, among other information. The union of all these triples, each of which has a verifiable pedigree, is accessible to both needs. RDF triples can be used to request and provide information that is needed or that has to be modified through the communication channel. Any state modification in the shared transaction (such as an alteration to the estimated arrival time) is also represented by the addition of new triples to the channel. Not just one, but several of these needs are controlled by an actor organising a larger portion of the transport chain. These needs are naturally merged in one RDF model that merely covers a larger portion of the transport transaction chain than the models available to each of the other participants. The remainder of this chapter describes the modifications needed to apply WoN to use cases involving transportation. The attentive reader will note that none of these subjects are particularly relevant to the transportation industry. Prior to tackling domain-specific functionality that addresses issues identified in our interviews, however, they must be resolved.

9.5. Supply Chain Service Descriptions

Entities exhibiting concrete interest in a transaction, such as a user offering a book for sale and another user seeking to acquire a book, are the fundamental building blocks of the WoN. Both users had the option of expressing their intent through a need. Both users would interact after receiving a hint message from a matching service. The transporter manages pick-up and delivery requirements.

Offerings for general services can be seen as factory requirements that are communicated to any new, possible transaction partner. For instance, if a courier service is being offered, the factory will be notified whenever a potential customer requests a package delivery. However, not just any service announcement should be disclosed to the client. They have previously expressed their need, and they anticipate receiving offers that are specific rather than just links to other services they might be interested in. The logic underlying the factory need is activated when a potential client is made aware of them, and it then makes a specific offer (possibly taking into account situational factors such as current traffic, concurrent requests, or available resources). The newly created need object, which establishes a connection with the client's need, serves as a representation of this concrete offering. In contrast to the symmetric case that had been achievable in WoN, which is a case in which both needs in a match are informed of the match, such a circumstance necessitates distinct matching logic. When a manufacturing requires something, only the factory should be informed. Due to this requirement, we expanded how matching functions in WoN such that both parties are notified by default, but a party may want to suppress both the counterpart's and its own notifications. The prototypical implementation of this change underwent functional testing. The ability to specify that others should not be informed of one's needs, while not a complete solution, may help to resolve the problem mentioned under 'Privacy'.

9.6. Logistics Information Requirements

The information used for matching is not always the same as the information required to carry out a transaction, as explained under 'false assumptions'. Sometimes, everything is available when the contest takes place. In other situations, more inquiries are required. Due to the fact that both sides have access to the whole data transferred between participants, including their initial requirement descriptions, these data can be queried to determine whether or not the necessary information has already been provided. A participant may define information requirements in a declarative manner based on that system attribute. The information requirements are automatically checked when a connection is formed, and any missing information is noted. These data can be used by user interfaces to create interface elements (like forms) that will elicit the missing data. User agents might be able to automatically fill in blanks from personal data repositories. We need to be able to formulate and check them automatically in order to implement a system that enables participants to define their information requirements. For this component of WoN, we want to use shapes constraint language (SHACL) (Knublauch & Kontokostas, 2017). The forms themselves are defined in RDF, and SHACL is a formalism for describing shapes that an RDF graph may be tested against. Any party having access to the conversation material can then compare the content to the shapes. This enables a need author to incorporate SHACL in the need description. It is far more flexible to transmit the information requirements (shapes) in declarative syntax as opposed to displaying a service-defined user interface (such as an HTML form); user agents can pick the user interface technology for gathering the necessary information from the user. Additionally, SHACL permits the reference of shapes from any web address, allowing for the reuse of shapes and providing a way to standardise various use cases as well as the development of such standards. The next step is a full prototype implementation.

9.7. Message Retraction

Information requirements have to function at a level above just exchanging simple messages; this level is sometimes referred to as the level of meaning exchange. Each new message adds to the conversation's meaning by adding its content (RDF triples arranged in named RDF graphs). Participants occasionally need to alter the meaning, for instance, to fix a mistake. As a result, the communication protocol permits a message to be designated as retracted by linking to a message that was previously included in the conversation. Only the participant's own previously transmitted communications may be revoked. Retracted communications cannot be retracted by themselves. The result of retracting a message is that its payload is ignored in subsequent processes. The functionality that relies on users making and correcting errors, such as the problems raised by 'digitalised communication', 'contract negotiation', 'appointments', and 'pricing negotiation', would benefit from this intended feature.

9.8. Distributed Transactions and Long-running Work

In order to successfully plan and carry out the transport, it is necessary to coordinate more than two parties, particularly in the setting of multi-modal transport. In addition to involving numerous stakeholders, such an endeavour can take weeks or even months to complete, from initial planning to final delivery. The idea of long-term work (Bocchi et al., 2003) makes sense for describing such processes because of both of these factors. We choose to model connected and potentially layered business participant activities using the protocol logic specified by WS-BusinessActivity (WS-BA). In such a plan, a need takes on the function of the WS-BA coordinator in relation to the needs that serve as potential solutions to the issue. In this proposal, that need acts as a WS-BA participant with respect to a higher-level aggregate node. It is feasible to employ server-side logic that is called for an incoming message after the obligatory logic implementing the basic protocol has been executed in order to realise such a necessity in WoN, in either role indicated by WS-BA. The WS-BA protocol specification's state machine is subsequently implemented in response to the requirement. Participants all have access to this common system of states and state-altering messages, which can be utilised at any time to ascertain and affect the state of the distributed work. One of the building blocks for an integrated appointment making sub-protocol that addresses the situation mentioned in 'appointments' may be the option to add sub-goals to an overall plan. This option could also be used to realise linked conditional needs that find a one-way freight and the return freight simultaneously as required by Finding 'return freight'. This feature has an experimental implementation that will be updated.

9.9. Expressing Technology User Agreement

A contract must be established between the two parties in order for transactions or ongoing activity to be legally binding. Theoretically, a spoken agreement suffices to meet this condition; nevertheless, in practice, contracts are written, and discussing their contents is a key step in the negotiation process. The term 'contract' negotiation suggests that all parties might benefit from a united approach to contract negotiations. Our technology creates a communication channel between the participants and preserves every message sent and received in a way that makes the message history clear and unalterable. Because it is always possible to determine who said what and in what order, it is a perfect medium for contract negotiations. We offer the option to send a special message designating earlier messages as proposals in order to support negotiation. The alternative is for the opposing party to reference the proposal in an accept message, resulting in an agreement. The accept message's uniform resource identifier (URI) serves as a marker for the agreement. Only the message history prior to the accept message is taken into account when determining the agreement's content. Retraction therefore has no impact on agreements. By sending a message proposing to cancel an agreement and the counterpart approving that request, they can be terminated by either party. The protocol has been designed but has not yet been put into use as of this writing.

9.10. The Digitalisation of the Humanitarian Aid and Logistics

The development of new technologies today has sparked a keen interest among governments, practitioners, and donors in how the technology may best support humanitarian efforts. Cash and voucher (C&V) aid has been expanding quickly in recent years, and many humanitarian organisations are beginning to implement this kind of initiative substantially as a substitute for in-kind aid (Kovács, 2014). A report from Overseas Development Institute (ODI) (2016) shows that in 2015, out of a total spending of 24 billion on humanitarian help, at least $1.9 billion was spent in the form of cash-based solutions, even if there is presently no systematic tracking of the amount of humanitarian assistance supplied in the form of C&V (51% cash and 49% vouchers). About two-thirds of the total came from United Nations agencies, while just under a third came from non-governmental organisations (NGOs). Many of the top humanitarian organisations and donors announced a number of commitments to use more cash-based programming during the World Humanitarian Summit in 2016 (ODI, 2016). If C&V programming seems like anecdotal evidence to someone unfamiliar with humanitarian relief, it is vital to demonstrate how the digitalisation of aid through C&V implies a shift in the way humanitarian logistics are thought about. Traditional humanitarian aid has historically relied on an ultimate supply chain, as explained by Mentzer et al. (2001), starting with the needs analysis and ending with the recipients' distribution. The C&V programming significantly departs from this established model by handing off all downstream logistics operations to regional traders. Thus, the

C&V programming implies that for NGOs to transition from a new financial and digitalised assistance to a traditional in-kind assistance, this is a transition from physical flows management in the past to information flows management in the future.

This study attempts to comprehend what kind of effects the C&V programmes might have in the context of a prospective revolution for NGOs by offering the following research question: How might C&V programmes change how humanitarian NGOs handle their logistics? One of the authors who works in the field as a logistician noticed the quick changes occurring in the humanitarian sector, which sparked this investigation. Additionally, practitioners frequently address this subject in the various platforms for logistics coordination because they believe that they need to redefine the logistics function because a new kind of help is challenging their current role (Logistics Cluster, 2014).

9.11. Towards Another Digitalised Logistics: The Event Management

Since the e-cash and e-vouchers programmes are new to both practitioners and scholars, it is challenging to assess how they might affect the logistics of humanitarian aid. However, one nearby industry that is currently experiencing digitalisation in a manner similar to that of humanitarian relief may be used as an example. The event management industry has been known for utilising information technology more and more over the past several years. To demonstrate this point, let's focus on the music festival sector, which has been using cashless technologies since the early 2010s (Jackson, 2014). Humanitarian work and event logistics may appear to have quite different goals, stakeholders, 'clients', and other distinctions at first glance. The deep structures of these two businesses, however, are extremely similar, as demonstrated by Salaun (2017): a permanent structure with a huge network and a wide diversity of players to carry out transient initiatives (relief for humanitarian and festival for event). In reality, there are many similarities between the event logistics and the primary elements of the humanitarian logistics that were previously identified. According to Lexhagen et al. (2005) and Locatelli and Mancini (2014), 'operation excellence' in event management is one of the key elements to any event's success. Despite the fact that these authors don't provide a precise definition of 'operation excellence', it appears possible to link this idea to logistics. The logistics are critical in event management, just as they are in the humanitarian context. Additionally, according to Kerzner (2013), the inability to adhere to the event's schedule constraints and the challenges in meeting consumer requests owing to a lack of supplies are the two main causes of event failure. The short supply chain cycle and the scarcity of resources are two further commonalities between the event and humanitarian industries. Additionally, according to O'Toole (2000), event logistics have another trait that is similar to humanitarian logistics: operation management complexity brought on by a range of supply. These authors claim that event logistics and humanitarian logistics are very similar and are based on the same ideas. Due to the two logistics' close proximity, it is possible to draw the following simple conclusions. Event logistics and humanitarian logistics are extremely similar. The cashless innovation has and will continue to have an impact on event logistics. Given the similarities with event logistics, innovations may potentially affect humanitarian logistics.

Before moving forward with this concept, it is crucial to define cashless payment systems and discuss the significant effects they have had on music festival event planning. The cashless system has been in use for 10 years (Jackson, 2014), and it consists of a virtual wallet that is unique to each festival-goer. This virtual wallet, which is manifested by an RFID or NFC tag on a card or bracelet, is connected to festival-goers' bank accounts and allows them to add funds to it at any time. A festival-goer uses his RFID tag to pay for purchases by presenting it to a terminal (Dowson & Bassett, 2015). Only two studies have investigated the effects of becoming cashless on event logistics. First one, led by Jackson (2014), demonstrates how the absence of cash generates new information flows. The second, led by Salaun (2017), focusses on how the cashless system might affect the logistics strategy for festivals in three areas: (1) logistical processes; (2) warehousing; and (3) flows management (3). According to Jackson (2014) and Salaun (2017), the cashless system has had a significant impact on music festival management's logistics strategy and fostered innovative logistical techniques including subcontracting logistics service providers (Salaun, 2017). It would be useful to use the example of the cashless on event logistics to examine the potential effects of C&V programmes on NGOs' logistics strategy: a large logistical revolution followed by a little digitalisation.

9.12. Blockchains in Logistics and Supply Chain Management

Blockchain is an emerging technology idea that makes it possible to store verifiable data in a decentralised, unchangeable manner. Different industries have become more interested in it during the past few years. Blockchain is touted as the panacea that might replace the way that payments are handled and delivered now, particularly in the Fintech industry. The logistics and SCM community is slowly realising the potential impact that blockchain technology could have on their sector. To shed light on this emerging field, an online survey was conducted and on logistics professionals for their opinion on use case exemplars, barriers, facilitators, and the general prospects of blockchain in logistics and supply chain management. Participants have a generally favourable opinion of this new technology and its advantages. However, the judgement of the participants is significantly influenced by elements such as the hierarchical level, blockchain experiences, and industry sector. We believe that in order to make a relatively conservative business like logistics more enthused about blockchain, the advantages over current IT solutions must be more properly outlined and use cases must be further investigated.

Blockchain technology is used worldwide. It was created by Satoshi Nakamoto, one or more enigmatic figures who remain unidentified to this day. For the most of its history, it has been more of an insider's secret. Nine financial institutions, including Goldman Sachs, Barclays, J.P. Morgan, and others, teamed up to create a new blockchain-based financial services infrastructure, which was made public in September 2015. (Underwood, 2016). By that time, blockchain had emerged as the newest Fintech fad, with new startup and corporate projects being announced virtually every day. It took some time for the logistics and SCM community to catch on and begin to understand the potential effects of blockchain on their sector. One of the main goals of blockchain is to increase transparency by giving each network member access to the same information and creating a single source of truth (Tapscott & Tapscott, 2016). One of the most crucial and challenging areas for logistics and SCM improvement is supply chain transparency (Abeyratne & Monfared, 2016). It is not surprising that some logistics experts believe that blockchain has 'enormous potential' (O'Marah, 2017), will 'change the supply chain and disrupt the way we manufacture, market, purchase, and consume our commodities' (Casey & Wong, 2017), and will 'revitalize the economy' (Dickson, 2016). Blockchain could be the 'holy grail' when taken as a whole (Popper & Lohr, 2017). The enthusiasm around blockchain, however, appears to be mostly fuelled by technology suppliers, consultants, and journalists, as is frequently the case with nascent technology. Logistics professionals, particularly those working for small and medium-sized businesses, claim to know nothing about blockchain (Kersten et al., 2017). This can be explained by the novelty of the technology as well as the dearth of use cases that convincingly demonstrate how blockchain is superior to current IT solutions. Blockchain research in logistics and SCM is still in its early stages (Zhao et al., 2016); therefore, it should consider potential applications (Yli-Huumo et al., 2016). The research questions that this chapter will attempt to answer are 'What possible uses of blockchain technology in logistics and SCM would be appropriate?' and 'Should blockchain in logistics and SCM be regarded a treat or rather a trick?' The rest of the chapter is organised as follows: we start by listing the fundamental characteristics of blockchain. Then, we present four use case examples that have been both theorised and applied. The results of an international study we performed within the logistics sector to look at the prospects of the four use cases as well as expectations and concerns about blockchain are then presented. We wrap up by going through the results and speculating on how the logistics sector may use blockchain technology in the future.

9.13. Basics of Blockchains

The blockchain is a distributed digital log of transactions that uses cryptographic techniques to prevent tampering (Pilkington, 2016). The three most crucial characteristics of a blockchain are included in this succinct explanation: decentralised, verified, and immutable. It is decentralised because there is no centralised infrastructure or central authority to establish trust; rather, the network is totally managed by its users. A transaction needs to be shared among peers in the peer-to-peer (P2P) network of the blockchain in order to be added to the ledger. The ledger is kept locally by each participant. It is then validated, because the members employ public–private key cryptography to sign the transactions before distributing them to the network. Consequently, they can only be started by the private key's owner. The fact that the keys are unrelated to the members' actual identities, however, allows them to maintain their anonymity. Its consensus algorithm makes it immutable. To create a new block, one or more transactions are gathered together. The transactions in the block can be verified by any member of the network. The new block is disregarded if there is no agreement regarding its legitimacy. Similar to that, if there is agreement that the transactions in the block are legitimate, the block is included in the chain. Each block generates a cryptographic hash. Each block also contains the hash of the previous block in addition to transaction details. This develops a chain of interdependent blocks that connects to the blockchain.

Retroactively changing a transaction on the blockchain would necessitate changing both the local records on the majority of network users' devices and the cryptographic hash of each subsequent block. A distributed system, like a blockchain, has advantages over centralised designs because it gives every network member access to the same, verifiable information. By doing away with the requirement for trust, it establishes trust between the parties. Without a reliable middleman, blockchain can track the transfer of assets between two parties. Digital currency, carbon credits, or other ownership documents are examples of such assets (Tapscott & Tapscott, 2016). The first use of the blockchain concepts, the Bitcoin Blockchain, only permits straightforward transactions. Additionally, the fact that blockchain has been error-free since January 2009 and currently has a market valuation of over 35 billion Euros demonstrates how dependable it is. On the other hand, centralised infrastructures are rapidly being breached; typical middlemen like banks or dating services offer several examples (Tapscott & Tapscott, 2016). Existing now are numerous more sophisticated blockchain systems. The majority of blockchain implementations are public (permissionless), while some are private (permissioned), where a single entity controls who has the ability to read and write (Pilkington, 2016). Some blockchain implementations allow for 'smart contracts' or blockchain-based software (Christidis & Devetsikiotis, 2016). Code-based conditions make up smart contracts. An easy example is the delivery of a package: a smart contract may be created so that the sender's payment is only released when the shipping company confirms the delivery in order to reduce the chance of a loss. This enables an automated transaction that is also documented and regulated. Be aware that blockchain has drawbacks in addition to its advantages (Laplume et al., 2016; Xu, 2016; Yli-Huumo et al., 2016). The majority come from the technology's early stages of maturity. Although these issues (such as limited throughput) must be resolved from a technology standpoint, they shouldn't deter potential users from assessing the advantages of the underlying ideas.

9.14. Blockchains in Humanitarian Logistics and SCM

Blockchain is thought to have a lot of promise for boosting business models and streamlining procedures in logistics and SCM, as was said in the introduction. However, only a few logistics specialists are aware of blockchain, and even fewer are actively working on implementation plans, according to a recent report on trends in logistics and SCM (Kersten et al., 2017). By introducing use case examples, we illuminate the potential of blockchain in this section. These examples

Table 9.1.   Summary of the Use Case Exemplars.

Advantage of Blockchains	Practical Example
Faster paper work processing	The shipping industry still involves a lot of paperwork. Freight documents like landing bill are prone to loss and fraud. These costs money and time
Identification of counterfeit products	Supply chain problems are evident in the pharmaceuticals industries. Face cancer drugs are now rampant. Customers need the right commodities
Product tracking	Provides a quick overview of where the products came from and where they are going
The IoT	Objects need to be equipped with sensors that generate and relay data along the supply chain

illustrate four key concepts that are currently being researched in both theory and practice. In addition, they represent just four ideas among the many unexplored possibilities. Additionally, they represent just four distinct concepts in a sea of uncharted possibilities. We selected them in an effort to create a comprehensive and varied image that would subsequently be utilised to research the potential applications of blockchain technology for logistics and SCM. The use case exemplars are summarised in Table 9.1. The sections that follow give a more thorough introduction to each.

9.15. Ease of Paperwork Processing Freight Transportation

International container movements are accompanied by a thick paper trail. For instance, moving refrigerated items from East Africa to Europe needs the stamps and approvals of about 30 individuals and organisations, and there must be over 200 interactions between them. Additionally, documents like the bill of lading may be fraudulently obtained (Popper & Lohr, 2017). It is projected that the expenses of processing trade-related paperwork will range from 15% to 50% of the price of physical conveyance (Groenfeldt, 2017; Popper & Lohr, 2017). In 2015, IBM and Maersk teamed up to address such process inefficiencies and digitise paper records. The massive global network of shippers, carriers, ports, and customs was ultimately connected using a permissioned blockchain technology. The specifics of implementation still need to be worked out. However, a 2017 set of pilots was successful. Every pertinent document or approval was shadowed on the blockchain in these trial projects, which means the existing IT systems were enhanced rather than replaced. Every partner is given the ability to have complete visibility of the container status via a common interface (Allison, 2017). By the end of 2017, Maersk intends to track 10 million boxes per year, or one in every seven of their container shipments on the blockchain (Groenfeldt, 2017). The issues brought on by copious documentation don't just affect this use case; they affect all commerce movements (Chu et al., 2016; Morabito, 2017).

9.16. Identifying Counterfeit Products

High-value products' provenance frequently depends on paper certificates, which can be misplaced or altered. Determining whether a diamond's certificate is real or fraudulent and whether the diamond was stolen is not always simple. The same is true for pricey purses, watches, and wine (Lomas, 2015). Since a diamond's serial number, for instance, can easily cut, the startup Everledger adopts a different strategy and stores 40 data points that individually identify a diamond. A prospective purchaser may easily identify whether the vendor is the true owner of the diamond using these openly accessible blockchain records, and they can also ensure that they are not purchasing a 'blood diamond' that was mined in a conflict area (Underwood, 2016). This fraud detection technology will be expanded by Everledger into a provenance platform for numerous expensive items (Lomas, 2015). In the medical field, fake medications are a well-known issue that, in the case of anti-cancer medications, can even prove fatal if patients do not follow the recommended course of therapy (Mackey & Nayyar, 2017). By establishing supply chain transparency from manufacturers via wholesalers and pharmacies to individual patients, blockchain could increase patient safety. Patients could be given the ability to verify that they received the correct medications through the use of barcodes or auto ID technology (DeCovny, 2017; Mackey & Nayyar, 2017). Blockchain is thought to make it far more challenging to tamper with items or introduce goods of questionable provenance (Apte & Petrovsky, 2016; Morabito, 2017; Sutherland et al., 2017).

9.17. Industry 4.0 and Tracking

Retailers struggle to identify the sources of the contaminated ingredients and the outlets to which they were shipped when faced with an epidemic of a foodborne illness (Tian, 2016). Today, locating the source of the contamination and restoring customer faith in food safety might take weeks (Popper & Lohr, 2017). Walmart and IBM teamed up in 2016 to make origin tracing for food items easier. Similar to Maersk, supply chain partners use Blockchain to supplement their current IT infrastructure by tracking the transit of food through a transparent, superior ledger. This open forum is thought to be a significant improvement over Walmart's past attempts with barcodes or auto ID technologies, which called for centralised databases and participant trust (Hackett, 2016). Walmart and IBM tracked domestic movements of pork from small Chinese farmers to Chinese stores as well as international movements of food from Latin America to stores in the United States using digital tracking in certain early trial projects (Popper & Lohr, 2017). In these pilots, information about the origin of the farm, batch numbers, manufacturing and processing data, expiration dates, and shipment details was recorded on the blockchain and made instantaneously accessible to all network users. With an outbreak of a foodborne illness, Walmart can quickly identify the source thanks to these data. More pilots with more data qualities are scheduled throughout the year. Walmart concludes that if the newly available data on shelf life is used as a criterion for supply chain optimisation, blockchain might also cut food waste (Shaffer, 2017).

9.17.1. Humanitarian Logistics Routeing

Routing enables on time delivery, real-time tracking, and the ability to on an appropriate delivery window. By organising their delivery procedures better, the shipper and the client can reduce congestion on delivery platforms. The installation site can set up its processes for on-time or late delivery thanks to better real-time routeing information made possible by the collection of real-time IoT data and Industrial Data Space (IDS)-based routeing algorithms (from the carrier to the logistics service provider and the client). Real-time rerouting enables the reduction of lateness in the event of disturbances.

9.17.2. Humanitarian Logistics Tracking

Through various IoT sensors connected to the package and the components inside, all packages and containers are able to communicate their location and condition.

9.17.3. Humanitarian Logistics Security

For a variety of uses, all data collected throughout the delivery process are saved on a secure blockchain. The locations and conditions of the containers' transportation during the delivery phase must be noted and safely kept. Once put together, the operating history can cover the entire lifecycle, including the recycling process at the end of the lifespan, and be kept on the same blockchain. Integration: To ensure that the logistics platform can cooperate with legacy solutions and with specified formats, existing transport management systems and mobile apps can be incorporated.

9.18. Operations and the IoT in Humanitarian Logistics

The term 'anything with a plug' refers to ordinary objects that are connected to the internet, have electronics installed, and can communicate with one another online. According to a Gartner research, by 2020 there will be more than 20 billion connected items (Gartner, 2015). However, the server infrastructure of the current internet architecture might be unable to handle such a volume of devices and data (Eastwood, 2017). Single servers pose a risk to data security since they are a single point of failure. IoT device connectivity and management are being looked at as potential solutions using the open blockchain ledger (Christidis & Devetsikiotis, 2016; Pilkington, 2016). Logistics may be one of the most promising uses for IoT and blockchain given the enormous number of potential IoT devices (vehicles, shipments, etc.) (Zheng et al., 2017). Large corporations are the first to work in this field. As an illustration, Walmart has received a patent that promises to enhance last-mile logistics by integrating delivery drones with the blockchain (Hackett, 2017). Such blockchain-connected IoT gadgets might also be given access to a digital currency. They would be able to communicate with others autonomously and use smart contracts to pay fees and duties on their own, such as for priority access to regulated air routes (Christidis & Devetsikiotis, 2016; Laplume et al., 2016).

9.19. Prospects of Blockchain in Logistics and SCM

A few research offered insightful information on the use of blockchain in the context of logistics and SCM. Despite being aware of the potential influence blockchain could have on their industry, businesses appear reluctant to invest resources in researching potential blockchain applications. In addition, the results

Table 9.2. The Supply Chain at the Centre of the Digital Enterprise.

Digital Work Space	Digital Manufacturing and Engineering	Digital Supply Chain	Digital Products and Services and Business Models	Digital Customer and Channel Management
DIGITAL APPLICATIONS				
Digital HR, E commerce and finance and knowledge sharing	Optimisation of big data processing	Procurement 4.0	Digital business models	Digital customer experience
	Predictive maintenance	Smart warehousing	Automated and data-based services	Omnichannel sales integration
	Horizontal and vertical integration	Autonomous and B2C logistics	Digitally enhanced products	Customer lifetime value management
	Condition monitoring	Prescriptive supply chain analytics	Intelligent and connected products and solutions	B2B2C customer interaction
	Integrated digital engineering	Integrated planning and execution		Point of sale driven replenishment
	Digital factory			
DIGITAL ENABLERS				
TECHNOLOGY, PROCESS, ORGANISATION				

shed light on the opinions of various participant groups. Our data reveal that middle managers are substantially less enthused about blockchain than c-level executives or operational staff when the hierarchical level of the participants is taken into account. They see fewer beneficiaries, predict more showstoppers, and rate the likelihood of blockchain adoption and benefit for the use cases far lower. For instance, 60% of middle managers express concerns about data security, compared to 28% of c-level executives. This lack of enthusiasm may be explained by middle managers' superior knowledge of their systems. Since they are probably in charge of putting new IT solutions into place (at least from the standpoint of the business), they might think blockchain is overhyped and is simply another IT advancement that is hailed as the panacea. According to our statistics, there are considerable discrepancies between consultants and scientists and logisticians who work for manufacturers, merchants, and logistics service providers. In terms of adoption obstacles and benefits, these discrepancies are startling. Logisticians struggle to understand the advantages and use cases, and consultants and scientists are concerned about how blockchain is developing technologically. Findings highlight the significance of identifying potential use cases for SCM and logistics. If workers from a traditionally conservative sector, like logistics, are to adopt new technology, the advantages must be very obvious. Logisticians tend not to get very enthused about new things.

The level of blockchain experiences is a third point of differentiation. The research suggests that participants' opinions of blockchain are more favourable the more experienced they are (e.g. studying use cases rather than merely observing the progress in the industry). We observe rising assessments of benefit and likelihood of adoption over the four levels of experience. Additionally, people with more experience identify more beneficiaries. Their viewpoint on potential obstacles changes: a high level of collaboration and dedication may be a barrier, according to about 60% of participants with implementation experience, compared to only 25% of participants with minimal implementation experience. Findings demonstrate the importance of conducting small-scale blockchain application tests to comprehend the limitations and advantages of the technology. Logisticians should conduct experiments to determine whether and how blockchain might benefit their own business.

9.20. Digitised Supply Chains and Humanitarian Logistics

Along with significantly reducing manual labour, digitised logistics integration makes it possible to develop new strategies for streamlining logistics operations and transportation routes. It also permits real-time monitoring of transportation flows so that quick responses to unforeseen events are possible. Because of this, including the most recent ICT has the potential to significantly increase logistics cost effectiveness and enable new business models based on real-time economics. Around 70% of businesses today lack information on operational performance across the whole value chain (World Economic Forum, 2016). The long-term objectives and related roadmaps of the European Technology Platform ALICE (cf. etp-logistics.eu) aim at a 10–30% increase in efficiency in the EU logistics sector, which would result in a 100–300 billion Euros cost reduction for the European industry. This is done to address the issue within the EU. In addition to increasing business competitiveness, a truly 'people, planet, and profit' oriented logistics and supply chain sector also helps to achieve environmental policy objectives. The involvement of several independent parties is one of the logistics industry's major issues (freight forwarders, third party logistic service providers, multimodal transport operators, carriers, etc.). The creation of a shared platform where all parties can communicate the necessary pertinent information is required in order for communication between these parties to be correct. Several prior EU-funded research projects (such as CONTAIN, FREIGHTWISE, e-FREIGHT, or i-Cargo, cf. containproject.com, freightwise.tec-hh.net, and eutravelproject. eu), as well as more recent commercial companies like Uber Freight, have made attempts to create such a platform. The issue with using such strategies is that an organisation must manage the shared platform. While having platform domination frequently offers the corporation controlling the platform a strong financial opportunity, other actors are required to pay fees and adhere to the whims of the platform owner. A single gatekeeper also puts the market's variety and fairness at risk. On the other hand, the risk of a fragmented market leading to suboptimal logistical decisions in distinct silos is increased by the presence of numerous rival platform businesses. A different approach – on which this work is focussed – is to handle logistics management in a P2P manner. Although crowd-sourced transportation is frequently referred to as P2P logistics, this chapter focusses on the traditional transportation sector. The logistics management system is completely distributed among the computational resources, which is the core of our P2P methodology.

The end result is a distributed system with a network of party interactions. The proposed framework aims to use and integrate two recent P2P technologies, including IDS, created at the Fraunhofer Institute in Germany, and blockchain, which was once a crucial component of cryptocurrencies (Banerjee & Mukhopadhyay, 2016), but is now considered to be a separate technology. The suggested P2P strategy prevents market monopolies, guarantees equal opportunity for participants of various sizes, and prevents vendor lock-in. The cloud-enabled transport management system is dispersed across numerous players in accordance with their processing capacities, which is the core concept of the newly proposed P2P platform. The end result is a distributed system with a network of actor–entity interactions that makes it possible for creative and smart data-based services.

Finally, we suggest a totally P2P design for logistics management that transcends the paradigm of a centralised platform. The platform combines three cutting-edge technologies: IoT, blockchain, and IDS. Although each of these technologies has been tried and tested in a different industry, they have never been merged in the way that they are now. As a result, the suggested system offers the logistics industry a completely new management strategy and creates opportunities for new inventions and enterprises to use this platform.

The crucial question is how can a P2P-based logistics management system contribute to and create new value in the digitised supply chain while resolving the tension between interoperability and data sovereignty? Although the technical elements we discuss in this chapter have been looked into in a number of contexts, including logistics, they have never been integrated into logistics as a means of enabling smart and creative data-based services. It's vital to keep in mind that while some businesses are already advertising P2P logistics services (such as p2plogistics.co.uk), they are only utilising a centralised client–server architecture platform to match the transit requirements with crowd-sourced providers. P2P approach concepts were initially envisioned on a broad level in a Hewlett-Packard patent, but their application to logistics has not yet been thoroughly researched or tested.

9.21. Humanitarian Logistics in Industry 4.0 Literature

A recent survey conducted by Sternberg and Andersson (2014) provides a thorough summary of the body of knowledge on distributed freight management. Decentralised intelligence in logistics, in particular, can be seen as a disruptive architectural breakthrough functioning at an IT infrastructure level, demonstrating significant network effects that have not yet realised, according to the authors. Reaching the necessary number of adopters is one of the main challenges identified by Sternberg and Andersson, who also stress the significance of industrial experiments.

The Fraunhofer Institute and the Industrial Data Space Association have developed the reference architecture and technologies for IDS (cf. industrialdataspace.org). The association presently has more than 50 members, including large corporations like DB Schenker, ThyssenKrupp, Schaeffler, FESTO, Bosch, SICK, Salzgitter, and SMEs like Setlog and Quinscape. Members also represent industries like manufacturing, production, logistics, ICT, and services. Ten or more European IDS centres are now conducting tests with IDS technology. The major German standardisation organisation DIN and ISO are currently standardising the IDS connector software component, which enables safe data transfer and processing, in a fast track method. IDS is acknowledged by the EU's digitising European industry initiative as a vital enabler for upcoming industry platforms (European Commission, 2016; Jarke & Pfeiffer, 2017).

The use of blockchain in various industrial and logistical applications is now being extensively researched as a result of Yuan et al.'s (2016) recent contribution, which makes the assertion that blockchain can revolutionise intelligent transport systems. Blockchain has already been used in various R&D initiatives and scholarly studies to improve logistics. For instance, IoT and blockchain are combined by Zhang et al. (2017) to offer a unique business model for IoT services, Apte and Petrovsky (2016) examine the deployment of blockchain within pharmaceutical supply chains, and so forth. In order to create a traceable agri-food supply chain, Tian (2016) integrates RFID and blockchain. The difficulties posed by the incorporation of blockchain in supply chain systems are examined in a recent contribution by Korpela et al. (2017). However, for a global integration within a supply chain context, a common standardised data model is additionally required to secure the interoperability, which is handled by the IDS technology in the platform proposed in this contribution. Blockchain design functionalities are shown to support good integration for ledger and smart contracts. In a nationwide project in Finland, blockchain technology and several related industrial business applications are now being examined (BOND – Blockchains bOosting FiNnish InDustry, cf. vtt.fi/sites/BOND).

The integration of blockchain open logistics APIs and related new business models for open transportation ecosystems are being worked on by a Scandinavian consortium (DBE Core; see dbecore.com/portfolio/what-next). The EU-funded research project SmartLog (cf. kinno.fi/en/smartlog) is now looking into the first Proof-of-Concept implementation for a solution incorporating blockchain and IoT in the logistics sector. According to Gartner, the business opportunities created by the advent of IoT offer a significant market prospect for the next 10 years (Jay & Rivera, 2014). Papert and Pflaum (2017) make suggestions for how logistics companies may use IoT. One of their main conclusions is that, in order to facilitate communication between various applications, the IoT platform should be built on open interfaces and open source software. Recent studies on various applications of IoT to logistics, transportation, and cars are available (Diaz Martinez et al., 2017; Xu et al., 2014; Guerrero-Ibanez et al., 2015; Guo et al., 2017). The blockchain technology is currently widely used in digital currencies, while additional use cases are still being developed in terms of technology readiness level (TRL) (TRL5). Industrial pilots employ IDS connector technology (TRL5). For a long time, positioning and other IoT sensing technologies have been used in production (TRL9). For the management of logistics systems, the combination of IDS, blockchain, and IoT has not been thoroughly proved in industrial use (TRL5).

9.22. Decentralised Value Chain Operations

The main goal of this contribution is to use cutting-edge P2P technology to make it possible to build a reliable, decentralised logistics infrastructure. Data sharing between the many participants in the logistics chain is made possible by IDS technology. Data governance, which makes it possible for parties to collaborate without disclosing sensitive information to one another, is a key feature. IDS connectors are able to decentrally implement any kind of customised algorithms, such as those for matching transportation choices to consumer needs or combining procurement systems.

9.23. Multi-modal Routeing Algorithms

The suggested platform enables the creation of cutting-edge static and dynamic algorithms for the best multi-modal transport choices. Utilising the aforementioned ICT does really make it easier for diverse parties to share data and information, which allows for wiser decision-making. Shorter transportation routes, higher vehicle load factors, reduced empty runs due to better route planning, shorter lead times, and subsequently lower inventories are all aspects of more effective logistics. As a result, transportation expenses will be reduced. Better load combinations and higher load factors, better route selection, and the unique benefits provided by the various modes of transportation (such as the flexibility of trucks, the reduced environmental impact of railroads, the lower costs of maritime transport, etc.) all contribute to the resulting financial savings, which in turn helps to shorten freight delivery routes and lower CO_2 emissions. Thus, all of these factors will also favourably affect the logistics system's ecological footprint. A unified stack of standardised technologies is a key facilitator for the rapid development of a many integration model, as stated in Korpela et al. (2017). The architecture of blockchain technology, including its design features and functionality, is generally standardised, which has made it easier to utilise in conjunction with other internet technologies. Utilising common IDS connectors, our platform implements IoT connection.

9.24. Conclusion

In order to achieve a significant degree of automation, the logistics 4.0 paradigm can be summed up as the optimisation of inbound and outbound logistics, which must be supported by intelligent systems, embedded in software and databases from which pertinent information is provided and shared through IoT systems. Furthermore, logistics may be viewed as a network where all processes can interact with one another and with people to improve their analytic capabilities across the supply chain. The supply chain will become smarter, more transparent, and more efficient at every point thanks to the digital transformation and the usage of intelligent, collaborative technology. New models that are more closely aligned with specific client needs will receive special attention, encouraging a marked improvement in the quality of decision-making as well as new levels of flexibility and efficiency in the near future. A multi-layered framework will be created in the future with the identification of the many stages, procedures, technical needs, and levels of integration, as well as the procedures for incorporating stakeholders who can help.

9.25. References

Abeyratne, S. A., & Monfared, R. P. (2016). Blockchain ready manufacturing supply chain using distributed ledger. *Journal of Research in Engineering and Technology*, 05.
Airbnb (2022) Airbnb Q4 2022 and full-year financial results. https://news.airbnb.com/en-uk/airbnb-q4-2022-and-full-year-financial-results/AllGreen. (2019). *AllGreen*.
Allison, I. (2017). *Maersk and IBM want 10 million shipping containers on the global supply blockchain by year-end*.
Apte, S., & Petrovsky, N. (2016). Will blockchain technology revolutionize excipient supply chain management? *Journal of Excipients and Food Chemicals*, 7(3), 76–78.
Banerjee, A., & Mukhopadhyay, S. K. (2016). A contemporary TOC innovative thinking process in the backdrop of leagile supply chain. *Journal of Enterprise Information Management*, 29(3), 400–431. https://doi.org/10.1108/JEIM-08-2014-0086
Bizer, C., Heath, T., & Berners-Lee, T. (2009). Linked data-the story so far. *International Journal on Semantic Web and Information Systems*, 5(3), 1–22.
Bocchi, L., Laneve, C., & Zavattaro, G. (2003). A calculus for long-running transactions. In E., Najm, U. Nestmann & P. Stevens (Eds.), *Formal methods for open object-based distributed systems* (pp. 124–138). Springer.

Casey, M. J., & Wong, P. (2017). *Global supply chains are about to get better, thanks to blockchain.*

Christidis, K., & Devetsikiotis, M. (2016). Blockchains and smart contracts for the internet of things. *IEEE Access 4*, 2292–2303.

Chu, Y., Ream, J., & Schatsky, D. (2016). *CFO insights: Getting smart about smart contracts.* Deloitte.

Daniele, L. (2013a). *Logistics core ontology.* TNO. http://ontology.tno.nl/logico/

Daniele, L. (2013b). *Logistics services ontology.* TNO. http://ontology.tno.nl/logiserv/

Daniele, L. (2013c). *Transport ontology.* TNO. http://ontology.tno.nl/transport/

Daniele, L., & Ferreira Pires, L. (2013). An ontological approach to logistics. In M. Zelm, M. van Sinderen, & G. Doumeingts, ISTE Ltd (Eds.), *Enterprise interoperability, research and applications in the service-oriented ecosystem, IWEI'13 proceedings* (pp. 199–213). John Wiley & Sons, Inc. Retrieved July 07, 2017, from https://lists.w3.org/Archives/Public/semantic-web/2017Jul/0004.html

DeCovny, S. (2017). *Experts discuss tackling pharma supply chain issues with blockchain.*

Diaz Martinez, J., Ruiz Ariza, J., Contreras Salinas, J., & Hernández Palma, H. (2017). Technology management to increase the efficiency of the supply chain. *Journal of Theoretical and Applied Information Technology.*

Dickson, B. (2016). *Blockchain has the potential to revolutionize the supply chain.*

Digitising European Industry Initiative. (April, 2016). Coordinated action plan with Member States: Adopted on 7 December 2018.

Dowson, R., & Bassett, D. (2015). Event Planning and Management: A Practical Handbook for PR and Events Professionals (PR In Practice). Kogan Page.

Eastwood, G. (2017). *Why blockchain is the future of IoT.*

Garcia, A. (2015). *iCargo – Intelligent cargo in efficient and sustainable global logistics operations.* ATOS Spain SA. http://cordis.europa.eu/project/rcn/100869_en.html

Gartner. (2015). *Gartner says 6.4 billion connected 'things' will be in use in 2016, up 30 percent from 2015* [Technical Report].

Groenfeldt, T. (2017). *IBM and Maersk apply blockchain to container shipping.*

Guerrero-Ibañez, J., Zeadally, S., & Contreras Castillo, J. (2015). Integration challenges of intelligent transportation systems with connected vehicle, cloud computing, and Internet of Things technologies. *IEEE Wireless Communications, 22*, 122–128.

Guo, S., Shen, B., Choi, T.-M., Jung, S. (2017). A review on supply chain contracts in reverse logistics: Supply chain structures and channel leaderships. *Journal of Cleaner Production, 144*, 387–402.

Hackett, R. (2016). *Walmart and IBM are partnering to put Chinese pork on a blockchain.*

Hackett, R. (2017). *Wal-Mart explores blockchain for delivery drones.*

Hofman, W., Punter, M., Bastiaansen, H., Cornelisse, E., Dalmolen, S., Palaskas, Z., Karakostas, B., Gato, J., Garcia, J., Herrero, G., & Gonzalez-Rodriguez, M. (2016). An interorganizational IT infrastructure for self-organization in logistics: Situation awareness and real-time chain composition. *International Journal of Advanced Logistics, 5*(2), 101–115.

Jackson, C. (2014). *The lived experience to the popular music festival-goer* [Ph.D. thesis]. Bournemouth University.

Kersten, W., Seiter, M., von See, B., Hackius, N., & Maurer, T. (2017). *Trends and strategies in logistics and supply chain management – Digital transformation opportunities.* DVV Media Group.

Kerzner, H. R. (2013). *Project management: A systems approach to planning, scheduling, and controlling* (11th ed.). John Wiley & Sons.

Kleedorfer, F., Busch, C. M., Pichler, C., & Huemer, C. (2014). The case for the web of needs. In *2014 IEEE 16th conference on business informatics* (Vol. 1, pp. 94–101). IEEE.

Kleedorfer, F., Panchenko, Y., Busch, C. M., & Huemer, C. (2016). Verifiability and traceability in a linked data based messaging system. In A. Fensel, A. Zaveri, S. Hellmann & T. Pellegrini (Eds.), *Proceedings of the 12th international conference on semantic systems: SEMANTiCS 2016* (pp. 97–100). ACM.

Knublauch, H., & Kontokostas, D. (2017). *Shapes constraint language (SHACL) – Proposed recommendation* [Technical Report].

Korpela, K., Hallikas, J., & Dahlberg, T. (2017). Digital Supply Chain Transformation toward Blockchain Integration. 10.24251/HICSS.2017.506.

Kovács, G. (2014). Where next? The future of humanitarian logistics. In G. Heaslip & P. Tatham (Eds.), *Humanitarian logistics: Meeting the challenge of preparing for and responding to disasters* (2nd ed., pp. 275–286). Kogan Page.

Laplume, A., Petersen, B., & Pearce, J. (2016). Global value chains from a 3D printing perspective. *J Int Bus Stud*, *47*, 595–609. https://doi.org/10.1057/jibs.2015.47

Lexhagen, M., Nysveen, H., & Hem, L. E. (2005). Festival coordination: An exploratory study on intention to use mobile devices for coordination of a festival. *Event Management*, *9*(3), 133–146.

Locatelli, G., & Mancini, M. (2014). Controlling the delivering of projects in mega-events: An application on Expo 2015. *Event Management*, *18*(3), 285–301.

Logistics Cluster2014 Annual Report. https://logcluster.org/blog/logistics-cluster-2014-annual-report

Lomas, N. (2015). *Everledger is using blockchain to combat fraud, starting with diamonds.*

Mackey, T. K., & Nayyar, G. (2017). A review of existing and emerging digital technologies to combat the global trade in fake medicines. *Expert Opinion on Drug Safety*, *16*(5), 587–602.

Manola, F., & Miller, E. (2004). *RDF primer* [Technical Report].

Morabito, V. (2017). *Business innovation through blockchain*. Springer.

Nakamoto, S. (2008). *Bitcoin: A peer-to-peer electronic cash system.*

O'Marah, K. (2017). *Blockchain for supply chain: Enormous potential down the road* (pp. 626–629).

O'Toole, W. (2000). Towards the integration of event management best practice by the project management process. In *Event Beyond 2000*.

Overseas Development Institute. (2016). *Counting cash: Tracking humanitarian expenditure on cash-based programming* [Technical Report].

Papert, M., & Pflaum, A. (2017). Development of an ecosystem model for the realization of internet of things (IoT) services in supply chain management. *Electronic Markets*, *27*(2), 175–189.

Pfeiffer, A., & Jarke, M. (2017). Digital Transformation Within the Emobility Market -Learnings and Insights from Early Market Development. In C. Derksen & C. Weber (Eds.), Smart Energy Research. At the Crossroads of Engineering, Economics, and Computer Science. SmartER Europe SmartER Europe 2017 2016. IFIP Advances in Information and Communication Technology, vol 495. Springer, Cham. https://doi.org/10.1007/978-3-319-66553-5_2

Pilkington, M. (2016). Blockchain technology: Principles and applications. In F. X. Olleros & M. Zhegu (Eds.), *Research handbook on digital transformations* (pp. 1–39). Edward Elgar Publishing.

Popper, N., & Lohr, S. (2017). *Blockchain: A better way to track pork chops, bonds, bad peanut butter?*

Salaun, V. (2016). "La pérennité des Organisations Temporaires (OT) : compréhension du role conjoint de la pulsation organisationnelle et de la logistique - L'apport de l'étude des festivals musicaux -". PhD in Management. Aix-en-Provence: Aix-Marseille Université.

Salaun, V. (2017). Which evolutions of event logistics? The impact of cashless in music festivals. *Logistique & Management, 24*(3–4), 207–214.

Schwartz, J. D., Rivera, D. E. (2014). A control-relevant approach to demand modeling for supply chain management. *Computers & Chemical Engineering, 70*, 78–90, ISSN 0098-1354, https://doi.org/10.1016/j.compchemeng.2014.05.020

Shaffer, E. (2017). *Walmart, IBM provide blockchain update.*

Sternberg, H., & Andersson, M. (2014). Decentralized intelligence in freight transport—A critical review, *Computers in Industry, 65*(2), 306–313, ISSN 0166-3615, https://doi.org/10.1016/j.compind.2013.11.011

Sutherland, W. J., Barnard, P., Broad, S., Clout, M., Connor, B., Côté, I. M., Dicks, L. V., Doran, H., Entwistle, A. C., Fleishman, E., Fox, M., Gaston, K. J., Gibbons, D. W., Jiang, Z., Keim, B., Lickorish, F. A., Markillie, P., Monk, K. A., Pearce-Higgins, J. W., Peck, L. S., . . . Ockendon, N. (2017). A 2017 horizon scan of emerging issues for global conservation and biological diversity. *Trends in Ecology and Evolution, 32*(1), 31–40.

Tapscott, D., & Tapscott, A. (2016). *Blockchain revolution* (1st ed.). Penguin Random House.

Tian, F. (2016). *An agri-food supply chain traceability system for china based on RFID & blockchain technology* [Conference session]. 13th international conference on service systems and service management (ICSSSM) (pp. 1–6). 24-26 June 2016.

Uber. (2017). Uber Announces Results for Fourth Quarter and Full Year 2022. https://www.uber.com/.

Underwood, S. (2016). Blockchain beyond Bitcoin. *Communications of the ACM, 59*(11), 15–17.

UNECE. (1956). *Convention on the contract for the international carriage of goods by road (CMR)* [Technical Report]. United Nations Economic Commission for Europe (UNECE).

World Economic Forum (2016) Annual Report 2016-2017. https://www3.weforum.org/docs/WEF_Annual_Report_2016_17.pdf;

Xu, J. J. (2016). *Are blockchains immune to all malicious attacks? Financial Innovation, 2*, 25.

Xu, L., & He, W., & Li, S. (2014). Internet of Things in Industries: A Survey. IEEE Transactions on Industrial Informatics, 10, 2233–2243.

Yli-Huumo, J., Ko, D., Choi, S., Park, S., & Smolander, K. (2016). Where is current research on blockchain technology? A systematic review. *PLoS ONE, 11*(10), 1–27.

Yuan, Y., & Wang, F. Y. (2016). "Towards blockchain-based intelligent transportation systems," 2016 IEEE 19th International Conference on Intelligent Transportation Systems (ITSC) (pp. 2663–2668). Rio de Janeiro, Brazil. doi: 10.1109/ITSC.2016.7795984.

Zhao, J. L., Fan, S., & Yan, J. (2016). Overview of business innovations and research opportunities in blockchain and introduction to the special issue. *Financial Innovation, 2*, 28.

Zhang, M., Pawar, K., & Bhardwaj, S. (2017). Improving supply chain social responsibility through supplier development. *Production Planning & Control, 28*, 1–12. 10.1080/09537287.2017.1309717.

Zheng, Z., Xie, S., Dai, H.-N., & Wang, H. (2017). Blockchain challenges and opportunities: A survey. *International Journal of Electric and Hybrid Vehicles, 14*, 352–375.

Chapter 10

Humanitarian Logistics: The Way Forward

10.1. Introduction

Since the turn of the millennium, the area of humanitarian logistics has been the subject of a broadening array of studies aimed at enhancing both individual nations' and the global community's capacity to handle the challenges of anticipating and responding to natural and man-made disasters. From what Collins and Kapucu (2008) refer to as social, managerial, or technological viewpoints, the topic has been examined in these contributions. As a result, appeals have been made for the humanitarian logistic community to become more professional by improving personnel selection, training, and education (Thomas & Mizushima, 2005). Parallel to this, others have argued for the use of critical success factors (CSFs), operations research (OR) methodology, and performance measurement and management strategies (e.g. Balcik & Beamon, 2008; Pettit & Beresford, 2009; Schulz & Heigh, 2009). Technology such as geographic information systems (GISs) or unmanned aerial vehicle systems (UAVs) has been suggested as an approach to improve the requirements assessment process (Benini et al., 2009; Kovács & Tatham, 2009). Additionally, it is becoming more widely acknowledged that supply network information management systems have the potential to make managing the subsequent delivery of relief supplies less difficult (Bartell et al., 2006).

A large portion of this expanding academic interest reflects the elevated status given to supply network management (SNM) in the broader world of business and industry, as well as the rising understanding that the logistical components of emergency help provision are a significant cost driver. SNM may not be as well-known or understood as supply chain management (SCM), but we think it more accurately describes the reality that is present in many commercial and humanitarian contexts. This opinion is supported by other academics, including Chandra and Kumar (2000), Harland et al. (2001), Christopher (2005), and Aitken et al. (2005), and is illustrated by Lambert et al.'s (1998) observation.

As a result, conversations in this last chapter take place within the framework of a multi-organisational network that includes the transfer of material from its source to the ultimate recipients. In doing so, we take into account activities like the acquisition of supplies by assistance organisations, their delivery to the

Supply Networks in Developing Countries:
Sustainable and Humanitarian Logistics in Growing Consumer Markets, 129–143
Copyright © 2023 by Tatenda Talent Chingono and Charles Mbohwa
Published under exclusive licence by Emerald Publishing Limited
doi:10.1108/978-1-80117-194-620231010

afflicted area, and their distribution in the end. While we share many commercial companies' perspectives in this regard, we would also like to underline the ad hoc and ever-evolving character of the methods used to provide relief to individuals affected by a disaster. However, strictly speaking, the supply chain is a network of various businesses and interactions rather than merely a chain of companies having direct, business-to-business relationships.

10.2. Key Humanitarian Logistics Challenges

There are many difficulties awaiting the first responders and authorities in emergencies. According to Kovacs and Spence (2009), it is inevitable that choices will be limited. The global demand for humanitarian aid, including requests for help from national governments, continues to expand. The intensity of man-made and natural disasters has increased, conflicts have intensified, and vulnerabilities have dramatically increased as a result of the global financial crisis, rising food prices, energy and water shortages, unsafe virology experiments, population growth, bad politics and unorganised urbanisation. The effects of global warming can also be added to the list of potential challenges that humans face in their day-to-day life.

A significant number of the 350 or so natural disasters that occur annually around the world, mostly take place in nations that are least prepared, both economically and socially, to deal with them (Rodriguez et al., 2009). Thus, the 7.1 magnitude earthquake that hit Haiti in January 2010 caused an estimated 230,000 fatalities, which was more than quadruple the death toll from any other magnitude 7 event (Bilham, 2010). This was mostly brought on by pre-existing societal circumstances. Hence, in the growing consumer markets, humanitarian organisations and governments need to invest more in aspects of preparedness and mitigation, before disasters strike.

10.3. The Impact of Humanitarian Logistics Research

An interesting study that is also significant is what is meant by 'impactful research' (Cachon, 2012). Few of the many publications that have been published have had an impact, or actual use, in humanitarian organisations (Charles et al., 2010; Jahre et al., 2016; Kunz et al., 2015). Humanitarian organisations have increased their investment in logistics over the past 10 years as they have come to understand how crucial this role is to their operations. Humanitarian organisations may have pushed the topic up the agenda and attracted financing and talent by taking advantage of the growing scientific interest. As a result, they are able to hire and train more qualified individuals. Increasingly, program planners factor logistics into their scheduling much earlier, but this is still not always the case.

Since most humanitarian organisations now place a larger value on logistics, that is, getting aid to the victims, the industry is open to implementing fresh concepts, where thoughts should originate from the question, How can we get aid to the victims? Humanitarian groups need to adopt ideas and concepts from the business sector and this can be done mostly by engaging consultancy firms to join the market. Consultancy firms can help create customised systems that have the potential to have a significant impact on humanitarian logistics research (Deo et al., 2015).

Research on humanitarian logistics can be relevant in a variety of ways. We specifically pose the research questions below. (1) What obstacles prevent research on humanitarian logistics from being useful in practice? (2) How may the practice of humanitarian logistics research be improved? (3) What obstacles still need to be overcome, and what would be the best course of action? (Deo et al., 2015).

Combining perspectives from academia and practice can emphasise the importance of humanitarian logistics research. This has numerous benefits for both practice and research. It first deepens the understanding between donors, academics, and practitioners, the three groups that can gain a lot by cooperating. Setting the framework for future studies will be more helpful for humanitarian organisations in combining their needs with scholarly expertise and funds from funders, this may help the practitioners. This could lead to the definition of practice priorities, the adoption of joint research projects with funding from important contributors, the validation of results in the field, and widespread acceptance (Kovacs & Spens, 2009).

10.4. Humanitarian Logistics, Research, and Relevance for Practice

10.4.1. Poorly Defined Problems

Academics frequently begin their research by describing an issue that intrigues and appeals to them. This is affected by the researcher's preference for a specific strategy or topic. Researchers frequently prefer to exploit their areas of expertise. According to Gyöngyi Kovács (2005), they always want to employ a strategy that they are proficient at. These topics are not necessarily pertinent to humanitarian groups since researchers frequently have an inaccurate understanding of the problems faced by practitioners; hence, collaboration with various stakeholders is greatly encouraged.

Sigala et al (2022) argues that writing down the problem definition with the organisation in a formal document, like a term of reference, is still uncommon. If the organisation and the researcher do not discuss the topic in detail, there is no definition of how to judge whether the research effort was successful. If this is not specified at the outset of the study, there is a good probability that the researcher will simply pay attention to academic output, or the publication of a paper. As a result, it's possible to forget to turn the study's findings into suggestions the company can actually implement.

Furthermore, Sigala et al (2022) highlights that the timelines of researchers and charitable organisations differ. Sometimes there may be a three-year gap between data gathering and the publication of the next paper due to the length of the research procedure. Since their environment is so dynamic, humanitarian groups must begin new operations within months and end them within weeks. Given how quickly things change, it is not unexpected that humanitarian organisations cannot wait three years for an academic study's conclusions. Failure to create precise timetables and milestones early in the project frequently leads to frustration on the side of both parties.

10.4.2. Contextualisation Issues

Humanitarian organisations function in a very specialised environment that is extremely different from the one in which commercial businesses do. Logisticians working in humanitarian settings cannot rely on detailed plans because disasters are unpredictable. There is a lot of unpredictability in humanitarian logistics, the supply chain is not always as lean or agile as expected as forecasting is difficult in emergencies (Kunz et al., 2017). As a result, rather than thorough preparation, humanitarian logistics rely more on improvisation or dynamic adaptation. In contrast to commercial logistics, the main goal is take quick action to assist as many people as possible; sometimes with little thought, Humanitarian logisticians, however, continually have to strike a balance between rapid response and resource shortage. During disasters, established transportation infrastructure is frequently destroyed, forcing organisations to find alternate means to get supplies to victims. Convergence of organisations and goods to the catastrophe area is another characteristic of disaster environments, which increases the unanticipated difficulties of the response to a disaster. Holgun-Veras et al. (2012) explore these issues in great detail. Humanitarian groups are significantly impacted by the political climate in the nation where they are active. Humanitarian organisations must consider security issues in many nations since workers cannot move freely due to the threat of terrorism or kidnapping. Additionally, some host governments place constraints on aid agencies, such as through bad politics, corruption, draconian bureaucracy, and import restrictions on goods (Kunz & Gold, 2017; Kunz & Reiner, 2016).

Research sometimes produces results that are not practical for humanitarian organisations if some requirements of the humanitarian logistics setting are not considered. Logistics problems aimed at saving lives are essentially different than those in business contexts. Fresh perspectives and fresh hypotheses need to be generated. Some of the theory on typical supply chains is applicable and relatively evident. This should only be used as a foundation (Besiou & Van Wassenhove, 2020). Additionally, humanitarian organisation practitioners occasionally lack the abstraction skills necessary to apply a study's findings to their particular environment. They need to develop the ability to abstract their issues rather than concentrate on particulars. Humanitarian workers can also get insight from more general findings and acquire intuition they can use in their own situations.

10.4.3. Difficult Data Collection

Very few Databases exist with raw humanitarian data. It is difficult to find statistics in this area, which is a huge barrier for the humanitarian sector. The sector is still growing, and the fact that there are people in the field who are under a lot of stress, dealing with the disaster, experiencing it and may not have had the required training, as well as the fact that the victims and other donors might not be in a position to participate in surveys, makes it more difficult to collect data. Most donors and victims also like to remain anonymous. Thus, obtaining data is quite challenging (Besiou & Van Wassenhove, 2020).

Even when businesses gather data, it is sometimes not presented in the right way. The data are inaccurate, partial, or measured incorrectly, e.g. lead time does not account for order time. It may also contain errors. According to Besiou and Van Wassenhove (2020), data are frequently gathered solely for reporting and accountability purposes, which make them less than ideal for use in analysis and decision-making. Finding the appropriate level of data granularity is another difficulty. Humanitarian organisations frequently delay developing simple systems that could produce data good enough to serve the purpose of most decision-making and research until they have a complex system in place (for instance, GPS tracking of vehicles). In order to get the right data, researchers in humanitarian logistics frequently have to conduct their own data collection. It is challenging to gather data during a disaster response operation because disasters are unpredictable.

Data collection is challenging, and regrettably, some academics don't devote enough time to it, leading them to create models based on fictitious events. As they are not supported by empirical data and oversimplify issues, these methods can produce results that are irrelevant or even outright incorrect. Researchers should adhere to the fundamental rule of humanitarian action, 'do no harm'. Given the distinctive and usually complex dynamic setting of humanitarian missions, one must be cautious when making assumptions. To make sure that the recommendations are reliable and trustworthy, it is a good idea to close the loop by triangulating the findings (Besiou & Van Wassenhove, 2020).

10.4.4. Validation Issues

Researchers occasionally obtain data, conduct study, and publish their findings without first letting the organisation know. Sigala et al (2022) claims that certain humanitarian groups have reported learning that a document relevant to their work was published even though they did not approve it, and have never seen this before and that some of the conclusions are in fact incorrect. This draws attention to two risks connected to not sharing results with the company. First, the results might not be correct since the researcher might have erroneously assumed something or overlooked an important factor. Even though there are several statistical methods available to check the validity of the study methodology, these tests fall short of providing an assurance that the findings cannot be falsified. Cross-referencing the results with the experience of the practitioners involved in the study helps to ensure the accuracy of the initial hypothesis and interpretation of the findings. Second, after the study's results are published, the humanitarian group can disagree with them and request that the researcher change the results to fit its needs. Such behaviour is likely going to affect future cooperation.

10.4.5. Access to Research Issues

Access to published research on humanitarian logistics is scarce for humanitarian groups. Academic publishers charge readers to access papers, and copyright clauses prevent researchers from making their work available on repositories or private websites, so once a paper is published in an academic journal, humanitarian organisations and other academics cannot easily access it. According to Sigala et al (2022), typical humanitarian organisations and some academic institutions are unable to afford journal subscriptions for every publication where research on humanitarian logistics is published.

10.4.6. Trust Issues

Lack of trust between humanitarian groups and scholars has hampered studies on humanitarian logistics. Academics are frequently viewed by humanitarian workers as theoretical individuals with little understanding of the context and realities of humanitarian organisations. Humanitarian workers are frequently viewed by researchers as experts who learnt their trade on the job and have little background in the scientific principles they should be using (Besiou & Van Wassenhove, 2020).

Trust issues between academics and practitioners may also arise when a university sends PhD students or interns to a humanitarian organisation. Although the businesses favour highly educated and fairly cost workers, dependability issues or a lack of long-term commitment do arise periodically. Thanks to the confidence between the organisation and the institution, these worries are reduced and practitioners are satisfied that only reliable students are being offered. Professors must pick their students carefully when putting them to work for an organisation in order to build this trust. Before interns are placed with a company, Besiou and Van Wassenhove (2020) recommend giving them little projects to assess their skill level and make sure they won't do anything improper.

10.4.7. Communication Issues

Academics and practitioners could have problems communicating with one another since they sometimes speak different languages, claim Besiou and Van Wassenhove (2020). Researchers usually utilise highly technical terminology and fail to adapt to the communication style of their peers since there are little incentives for them to convert their findings into a managerial format that is valuable to practitioners. Practitioners may view this as being conceited. This just serves to increase mistrust. The fact that practitioners usually learned their skills on the job furthers this barrier. Due to their lack of experience engaging with academics, individuals may feel as though they are beneath scholars.

10.4.8. Academia, Humanitarian Organisations, and Competition

Duplication of research efforts has previously been caused by competition between academic institutions and humanitarian groups. It is not unusual for two universities with complementary fields of study to compete for access to a charity or even to work on related tasks separately without attempting to cooperate (Kunz et al., 2017). Humanitarian organisations are perplexed by this competition because they see it as a waste of resources and don't understand why two universities can't just work together on a project. In a similar vein, competition among humanitarian organisations harms research. Organisations are not always willing to share the results of a research project. Consequently, researchers may not be allowed to publish their findings in an academic journal to translate their research findings into a managerial format that is convenient for practitioners. This may come across as arrogant to practitioners. This serves to reinforce the distrust. This barrier is strengthened by the fact that practitioners frequently acquired their abilities on the job. They may feel as though scholars are looking down on them since they have no experience interacting with academics.

10.4.8.1. Context Recognition. To avoid selecting an unrelated topic or making incorrect assumptions, it is crucial to understand the specifics of the humanitarian setting. Academics must familiarise themselves with the relevant vocabulary, do extensive background study, consult with subject-matter experts, and more before starting this kind of research. Sigala et al (2022) asserts that postgraduate students should devote a significant amount of effort to studying the correct terminology because there are numerous terminologies related to humanitarian logistics and humanitarian operations. With this background knowledge, researchers can only undertake significant research that is relevant to humanitarian organisations. Although some researchers have past experience working for charitable organisations, it is clear that this background is not necessary to carry out useful studies.

It is clear that time spent learning about the context should only be spent by academics who can commit more time to this project in the long run. Therefore, if someone wants to learn about this topic, they need to do so for a while. You can't just walk in, do your thing, and walk out. The process of entering this area takes some time. One must go to the field to fully understand the issues and mindset of humanitarian workers. It is difficult for students to quickly assimilate because the environment is new and unstable. One needs to spend several years on it in order to fully understand (Besiou & Van Wassenhove, 2020).

10.4.8.2. Issues of Research Relevance. In order to preserve relevance, it is essential that academics and humanitarian practitioners define research programs together. Sigala et al (2022) asserts that defining an issue in conjunction with help organisations is the simplest method to find it. Since humanitarian organisations aren't always aware of the problems they encounter, they can benefit from a researcher's neutral viewpoint. The issue must be noted as soon as it is identified in a document like the terms of references. The terms of references need to be written very precisely (Kunz et al., 2017). Defining terms of reference is a challenging task. It needs a lot of my time and personal engagement because we have to pick the right speakers and themes (Besiou & Van Wassenhove, 2020). When possible, it is advantageous to work on research projects financed by humanitarian organisations because this ensures that the issue is relevant for practice and that the organisation will profit from the research's findings. When a research team works on a project that is supported by a charity, the charity is invested in the outcome, pays for it, and raises important issues that the project needs to solve. The good news is that it is their issue and not one that we think they have or that a student thinks would be a good fit for a linear programming method (Beisiou & Van Wassenhove, 2020). When working on a funded study, the researcher must, nevertheless, always keep their focus on the expected contribution to knowledge generation. If not, the project can have an excessively consulting-centric focus.

10.5. Humanitarian Logistics and Performance Metrics

Once a relevant issue has been selected, it is imperative to define exact measures. The ability to quantify actual performance with KPIs is something that is quite important. The ability to disclose the results is only one aspect of success; another is that the organisation's activities and impact on the beneficiaries are different. What goals does the study hope to achieve? What outcomes will a successful research project yield? How are these outcomes evaluated? These are important questions that must be asked right away if the researcher and the organisation are to agree that the project will be completed successfully. The researcher's notion of success would surely include publishing in a recognised journal. The implementation of the recommendations, the number of beneficiaries who benefited from the improvement, or the amount of money that was saved as a result of the research's recommendations may all be used to gauge the success of the humanitarian organisation. It's important to keep in mind, though, that the researcher has no control over how the research project is carried out. Even the best research may go unused and in a drawer due to a sudden change in the organisation's priorities or a staff change. Academics support the idea of defining KPIs for humanitarian logistics operations and research. It's a great idea, and it's obvious that the KPI should contain data on implementation, actual results, and publications. These KPIs, for instance, could be part of the project's terms of reference.

10.6. Humanitarian Logistics and Open Agendas

Academic institutions and humanitarian organisations should have open agendas and improve communication about their joint interests and objectives: The agendas should be very clear and displayed for everyone to see (Kunz et al., 2017). Sometimes both sides have erroneous notions of what the objectives of the other party are, which is detrimental to a partnership that is advantageous to both. Clear expectations will always promote transparency.

According to Sigala et al (2022), researchers in humanitarian logistics are typically driven by a desire to advance knowledge and aid those working in the field in providing aid to those in need. Additionally, they want to publish the findings of their research in scholarly journals. These magazines prioritise scientific contributions over anything that aid organisations might require. The academic community should inform the humanitarian group of these various goals and expressly pledge to support them both. It is important for humanitarian groups to acknowledge the study project's dual goals.

There are many objectives for humanitarian organisations in working with intellectuals. The basic objective is to find assistance to address a problem for the benefit of the receivers. However, some groups could also submit their selections for review by a research institution. Practitioners could have predetermined assumptions about how to approach a problem and seek external confirmation to support them. If the organisation is open with the researcher about these existing views, they can be taken into account in the research. However, it will guarantee that the researcher does consider all options before making his recommendations. There is no assurance that the researcher will get the results the company is looking for (Kunz, 2017).

10.7. Collaboration in Humanitarian Logistics

Building trust between academics and practitioners requires ongoing cooperation. Once a research team develops knowledge on a topic and an organisation, long-term collaboration has a number of benefits. First, the researchers' familiarity with the context, concerns, and difficulties of the organisation makes it easier for them to base their theories on reality. Second, it provides access to highly qualified experts who are familiar with academic research and the ability for researchers to get to know the organisation's staff members personally. Third, it is advantageous for the humanitarian organisation to have access to an objective, outside expert who might challenge the status quo (Sigala et al., 2022).

According to Sigala et al (2022), when conducting research with commercial companies, long-term connections are unquestionably advantageous. In the humanitarian context, where effective research endeavours frequently depend on close bonds between a researcher and a reflective practitioner interested in research, this is even more crucial.

10.8. Data Collection in Humanitarian Logistics

Data must be acquired through the organisation's internal systems or directly from the assistance workers through surveys or interviews because publicly available information in this field of study is limited. To access information from an internal database, there must be a high level of confidence in the organisation. Researchers can benefit from internal databases, but our experience shows that even organisations with the best IT infrastructure can suffer with bad data (Kunz et al., 2017).

When statistics are difficult to get, the only choices are interviews or surveys of aid workers. To guarantee commitment and availability from employees, management support is required. Surveys and interviews can typically be conducted over the phone. To publish the results in scholarly journals, surveys usually encounter a range of approach challenges like convenience sampling, poor response rates, and small sample sizes. It is challenging for a researcher to travel to a country where operations are being conducted since there could be costs and safety concerns. Additionally, the technique for acquiring data must be developed to minimise its load on the humanitarian organisation (Besiou & Van Wassenhove, 2020). Through cooperation between researchers and humanitarian organisations, the data collected should be made accessible to other parties. The data must be structured and made anonymous in order for others to use it to do this.

10.9. Importance of Validating Findings with Relief Organisations

Once researchers have their results, they should return to the organisation and communicate them to the study project participants. Early discussion of the findings raises the likelihood that the researcher is on the right track and did not make incorrect assumptions. It gives the company a chance to respond to preliminary findings and identify details the researcher might have overlooked. Early outcomes also allow the organisation to put findings into practice before the paper is finished. Such early adoption is advantageous for both the results validation procedure and the academic publication process (Besiou & Van Wassenhove, 2020).

Researchers should return to the organisation with a final draft of the deliverables once the study is complete. It is important to offer the organisation a chance to comment on this draft and make modifications as needed. The paper that will be submitted to an academic journal can then begin to be written. Before publishing, the organisation should have a chance to read the paper. The validity of the findings is increased by comparing them to the opinions of practitioners. Additionally, this procedure develops mutual confidence between the company and the researcher. The possibility that the organisation will agree to conduct another research project in the future rises when results are shared openly. It is undoubtedly a good idea to specify how the project's outcomes will be communicated with the business in the terms of reference (Besiou & Van Wassenhove, 2020).

10.10. Language Usage and Translation

The findings of the study must be communicated to the research project's humanitarian partner in a language that is clear to its managers and staff. The researcher must convey theoretical topics in plain language rather than utilising jargon in order to achieve this. The truth is that few practitioners have the time or the technical expertise to study a specialised academic paper and make effective inferences from it. Unfortunately, academics are not encouraged to devote time to these activities because many universities only value scholarly articles. Academics work diligently until their piece is accepted by a journal before they may relax and go on to something else that will result in a new publication since their major incentive is to publish their work. Instead, they should set aside time right away to produce a report and deliver it to the class (Kunz et al., 2017). This extra effort is made as a courtesy to the research project partner organisation to summarise findings for the larger humanitarian community.

10.11. Importance of Results Sharing and Dissemination

Results must be shared with the larger community after being published in a report or an academic publication. There is a need to transfer the concepts developed by the academic community, which has experience in the humanitarian sector and has developed a number that could be very helpful (Besiou & Van Wassenhove, 2020). The beneficial effect that numerous researchers in humanitarian logistics are attempting to achieve can only be possible with this.

It is difficult to disseminate research since the readers of scholarly journals must pay to view papers. Humanitarian groups cannot justify the cost of this. The information produced in humanitarian logistics should be disseminated through different means. One option is to establish a central repository for all of the subject's published research. There is a vast body of information, research, and publications on humanitarian logistics, all of which are entirely scattered. The previously completed work might be kept in a repository with straightforward metadata that aid organisations could use to find and search for publications. As a result, humanitarian groups would be able to locate researchers who have experience in the areas of their concerns and examine existing literature for solutions to their difficulties. Researchers from institutions with smaller funds (such as those in poor nations) may potentially profit from such a repository (Besiou & Van Wassenhove, 2020).

When a humanitarian organisation funds a study, it can be more challenging to share the results with the public because confidentiality agreements might forbid it. This makes sense in part because internal organisational issues may be revealed by the research findings. However, organisations should put aside their concerns and decide to share general findings as long as sensitive data are deleted or anonymised. It's critical to make this clear right away (Besiou & Van Wassenhove, 2020).

10.12. Coordination of Research Activities

It's important to coordinate the research activities of numerous colleges and non-profit organisations: It is necessary to pool additional resources in order to maximise them, in part because there are probably two studies on the same topic being conducted at the same time using potentially conflicting data. Since some competition among research institutions is always beneficial for expanding knowledge, coordination does not imply that this competition should be abandoned. Reaching a consensus on issues should take priority and the findings of multiple studies should be utilised (Besiou & Van Wassenhove, 2020).

Coordination of research efforts might be facilitated via a portal where universities can identify their areas of specialisation and humanitarian groups can submit their research needs. Using such a virtual marketplace to match research demands with research resources would be a step towards a more structured and transparent system. Through the platform, research groups could identify collaborator institutions with complementary fields of study. Humanitarian organisations with connected challenges may pool their assets and plan a collaborative research project. Another method for educating the academic community about the value of research is through communication channels like University's News newsletters (Sigala et al., 2022).

Greater cooperation between humanitarian organisations will improve research dissemination. For humanitarian organisations, collaboration on knowledge expansion in their field of expertise may be useful. The Fleet Forum, a group that aims to improve fleet management in the humanitarian sector, has this as its main objective (Sigala et al., 2022). Last but not least, donors should mandate that research project outputs be made available to the academic and humanitarian sectors in order to encourage collaboration.

10.13. Opportunities and Challenges for Humanitarian Logistics in Growing Consumer Markets

First, humanitarian organisations should do research in a more organised manner. Instead of allowing staff members to handle requests for research projects on an individual basis, they can create an internal focal point to manage all of them. The organisations would then be able to establish appropriate procedures, such as mandating that each project be specifically specified with terms of reference and performance indicators. Second, charitable organisations have to be more forthcoming with the findings of the studies they conduct. When results are shared with other organisations, the entire community benefits, including the victims of the disasters. Humanitarian organisations might collectively decide on the most pressing issues, which would then serve as a guide for researchers.

Despite these suggestions, there are still a lot of difficulties. To prevent universities from needlessly duplicating research by working on comparable topics with several organisations, coordination of research efforts is required. There are many ways that research groups can complement one another, and institutions could collaborate considerably more successfully. The idea of 'running in packs', as described by Van de Ven (2005) as 'entrepreneurs who simultaneously coordinate and compete with others as they develop and commercialize their innovation', might be adopted by academic institutions as 'entrepreneurs who collaborate and engage in competition with others at the same time they develop and market their idea' (Van de Ven, 2005). This is similar to how cyclists compete in the final sprint while working together to make an escape. Humanitarian research can use the running in packs model. To define the main issues to be investigated and to determine the capabilities and areas of expertise of each research institution, research institutions may find it advantageous to coordinate their efforts. When the challenges are well defined, various research teams may select to focus on related aspects of the same issue or compete to develop the best solution for a given sub-problem. This would prevent the current, unplanned competition from confusing humanitarian organisations and causing annoyance when masses of students or researchers ask for the same information. Additionally, it would prevent the repetition of efforts that waste resources.

If universities and humanitarian groups were to agree to create a platform that listed the research needs of practice and the research capabilities of universities, it is suggested that such collaboration may be realised. Competition between institutions might still exist, but it would do so in a more open manner and on more definite research initiatives. While we recognise the necessity for academic freedom, it would be helpful if scholars in this developing field of study communicated and worked together more frequently. In this way, wasteful duplication of effort and squandering of limited resources could be reduced. It is difficult to set up such a platform since it requires central coordination. Unfortunately, previous attempts in this direction failed since some universities were not keen on working together (Besiou & Van Wassenhove, 2020). The biggest organisations and research institutes could undoubtedly generate interest and join forces on such a platform if a donor organisation had sufficient influence and resources.

The need to convert the frequently extremely technical and occasionally complex academic language into a managerial report that practitioners can easily understand presents another challenge. Due to language barriers, a significant portion of research is currently unavailable to some humanitarian groups. The volume of relevant publications is always increasing, making it challenging for practitioners to find them. We advise translating this knowledge so that practitioners can use it. The time and resources necessary for this are not available to researchers alone. To develop two-page managerial summaries of the most pertinent studies, a professional writer who has some knowledge of academic research and the humanitarian community could be assigned the task. A large donor might choose to support this idea because universities and humanitarian groups are unable to pay for it, which would have a significant effect on the dissemination of knowledge from research into practice (Besiou & Van Wassenhove, 2020).

The last issue mentioned has to do with how easily accessible scholarly publications are. Humanitarian groups frequently cannot access existing research even if they have the technical expertise and the time necessary to do so because they do not have the necessary database subscriptions (Besiou & Van Wassenhove, 2020). The best course of action should be explored with publishers, but one possibility is a shared repository for already published papers. When the final drafts of their articles were ready, researchers may upload them to the repository using a set of well-defined tags and categories. This would make it possible for humanitarian organisations to locate and freely access documents that are relevant to their issues. Once more, financing from an outside source is necessary to set up and maintain such a repository. The European Commission has set up a comparable archive to disseminate outcomes from publicly financed research projects (OpenAIRE project). Such a repository might be built for exchanging research on humanitarian logistics with the aid of a sponsoring organisation.

10.14. References

Aitken, J., Childerhouse, P., Christopher, M., & Towill, D. (2005). Designing and managing multiple pipelines. *Journal of Business Logistics, 26*, 73–96. https://doi.org/10.1002/j.2158-1592.2005.tb00206.x

Balcik, B., & Beamon, B. M. (2008). Facility Location in Humanitarian Relief. *International Journal of Logistics: Research and Applications, 11*, 101–121. http://dx.doi.org/10.1080/13675560701561789

Bartell, A. L., Lappenbusch, S., Kemp R. B., & Haselkorn, M. (2006). Improving Humanitarian Relief Information and Communication Systems through Research. *2006 IEEE International Professional Communication Conference*, Saragota Springs, NY, USA, 2006, pp. 156–162. doi: 10.1109/IPCC.2006.320379.

Benini, A., Conley, C., Dittemore, B., & Waksman, Z. (2009). Survivor needs or logistical convenience? Factors shaping decisions to deliver relief to earthquake-affected communities, Pakistan 2005–06. *Disasters, 33*(1), 110–131. doi:10.1111/j.1467-7717.2008.01065.x.

Bilham, R. (2010). Lessons from the Haiti earthquake. *Nature, 463*, 878–879.

Besiou, M., & Van Wassenhove, L. N. (2020). Humanitarian operations: A world of opportunity for relevant and impactful research. *Manufacturing & Service Operations Management, 22*(1), 135–145.

Charles, A., Lauras, M., & Van Wassenhove, L. (2010). A model to define and assess the agility of supply chains: Building on humanitarian experience. *International Journal of Physical Distribution & Logistics Management, 40*, 722–741. 10.1108/09600031011079355.

Chandra, C., & Kumar, S. (2000). Supply chain management in theory and practice: A passing fad or a fundamental change? *Industrial Management & Data Systems, 100*, 100–114. http://dx.doi.org/10.1108/02635570010286168

Collins, M. L., & Kapucu, N. (2008). Early warning systems and disaster preparedness and response in local government. *Disaster Prevention and Management, 17*(5), 587–600. https://doi.org/10.1108/09653560810918621

Deo, S., Gallien, J., & Jónasson, J. O. (2015, July 2). Improving HIV Early Infant Diagnosis Supply Chains in Sub-Saharan Africa: Models and Application to Mozambique. http://dx.doi.org/10.2139/ssrn.2511549

Harland, C. M., Lamming, R. C., Zheng, J., & Johnsen, T. E. (2001). A Taxonomy of Supply Networks. *Journal of Supply Chain Management, 37*:21–27. https://doi.org/10.1111/j.1745-493X.2001.tb00109.x

Holguín-Veras, J., Jaller, M., Van Wassenhove, L. N., Pérez, N., & Wachtendorf, T. (2012). On the unique features of post-disaster humanitarian logistics. *Journal of Operations Management, 30*(7-8), 494–506.

Jahre, M., Arvidsson, A., & Wassenhove, L. (2016). Defining logistics preparedness: A framework and research agenda. *Journal of Humanitarian Logistics and Supply Chain Management, 6*, 372–398. 10.1108/JHLSCM-04-2016-0012.

Kovács, G. (2005). Supply chain collaboration for sustainability [Conference proceedings]. Business Strategy and the Environment Conference, pp. 1–17.

Kovács, G., & Spens, K. (2009). Identifying challenges in humanitarian logistics. *International Journal of Physical Distribution & Logistics Management, 39*(6), 506–528. https://doi.org/10.1108/09600030910985848

Kovács, G., & Tatham, P. H. (2009). Responding to disruptions in the supply network – From dormant to action. *Journal of Business Logistics, 30*(2), 215–229.

Kunz, N., & Gold, S. (2017). Sustainable humanitarian supply chain management— Exploring new theory. *International Journal of Logistics Research and Applications, 20*(2), 85–104.

Kunz, N., & Reiner, G. (2016). Drivers of government restrictions on humanitarian supply chains: An exploratory study. *Journal of Humanitarian Logistics and Supply Chain Management, 6*(3), 329–351.

Kunz, N., Van Wassenhove, L. N., Besiou, M., Hambye, C., & Kovacs, G. (2017). Relevance of humanitarian logistics research: Best practices and way forward. *International Journal of Operations & Production Management, 37*, 1585–1599.

Kunz, N., Van Wassenhove, L. N., McConnell, R., & Hov, K. (2015). Centralized vehicle leasing in humanitarian fleet management: The UNHCR case. *Journal of Humanitarian Logistics and Supply Chain Management, 5*(3), 387–404.

Lambert, D. M., Cooper, M. C., & Pagh, J. D. (1998). Supply chain management: Implementation issues and research opportunities. *The International Journal of Logistics Management, 9*(2), 1–20. https://doi.org/10.1108/09574099810805807

Pettit, S., & Beresford, A. (2009). Critical success factors in the context of humanitarian aid supply chains. *International Journal of Physical Distribution & Logistics Management*, *39*(6), 450–468. https://doi.org/10.1108/09600030910985811

Rodríguez-Angeles, A., D´ıaz, A.M., & S´anchez, A. (2009). Dynamic analysis and control of supply chain systems. In *Supply Chain the Way to Flat Organisation*. IntechOpen.

Schulz, S. F., & Heigh, I. (2009). Logistics performance management in action within a humanitarian organization. *Management Research News*, *32*(11), 1038–1049. https://doi.org/10.1108/01409170910998273-

Sigala, I., Sirenko, M., Comes, T., & Kovács, G. (2022). Mitigating personal protective equipment (PPE) supply chain disruptions in pandemics – A system dynamics approach. *International Journal of Operations & Production Management*, *42*, 128–154. doi:10.1108/IJOPM-09-2021-0608.

Thomas, A., & Mizushima. M. (2005). Fritz institute: Logistics training: Necessity or luxury? *Forced Migration Review*, *22*, 60–61. https://www.fmreview.org/education-emergencies/thomas-mizushima

Van de Ven, A. H. (2005). Running in packs to develop knowledge-intensive technologies. *MIS Quarterly*, *29*(2), 365–377.

Index

Printed in the USA
CPSIA information can be obtained
at www.ICGtesting.com
JSHW011324091123
51787JS00004B/17

9 781801 171953